Money Advice for Your Successful Remarriage

Money Advice for Your Successful Remarriage

Handling delicate financial issues intelligently and lovingly

Patricia Schiff Estess

ASJA Press
San Jose New York Lincoln Shanghai

Money Advice for Your Successful Remarriage
Handling delicate financial issues intelligently and lovingly

ASJA Press
an imprint of iUniverse.com, Inc.

For information address:
iUniverse.com, Inc.
5220 S 16th, Ste. 200
Lincoln, NE 68512
www.iuniverse.com

ISBN: 0-595-16909-0

Printed in the United States of America

Acknowledgments

I did not write this book in a vacuum.

Almost one hundred remarried couples shared portions of their lives with me. These couples are from cities and towns across the country—from Atlanta to Los Angeles, Boston to Phoenix. I chose them through recommendations but at random. All but six had been remarried for at least three years, and, at the time we spoke, claimed to have found ways of dealing with the financial challenges they had faced and were continuing to confront. They were extremely honest about the difficulties of coping with their finances in the midst of divided loyalties and a new and complex relationship.

Time is a rare and precious commodity for remarrieds, yet the couples I spoke with were generous with it, both during and after the formal interviews. Although they're not identified in the book, they will recognize themselves within these pages.

The truths of this book come from these remarried couples. At the time they were telling their stories, they didn't always realize that there were certain underlying themes that would crisscross all the reflections: trust, fairness, respect, and love. These themes permeated the talk of investments, bank accounts, financial chores, taxes, houses and estate planning.

My thanks to the legal and financial experts who spent time with me, sharing and checking information that would be of help to the remarried couples reading this book: Marcia Marshall, Peter Strauss, Mark Levinson, Sidney Weinman, Richard Victor, Susan Richards, Jacalyn F. Barnett, Patricia Raskob, Vicki and Russ Schultz, Marvin Strauss, Lynne Gold-Bikin, Ann Salo, Fern Topas Salka, Sandy Geller, Bill Munn, Randy

Kaplan, and Murray Lennard. Their aggregate knowledge and credentials are impressive.

And to the social scientists, researchers and students of remarriage and stepfamilies, many of whom have been quoted in the book, more thanks for helping me understand why people act the way they do: Dr. Kay Pasley, Reverend Dick Dunn, Dr. Barnard Frankel, Andrea Wohl, and Dr. Florence Kaslow. Special thanks to Linda Perlin Alperstein, a noted family counselor and childhood friend, with whom exploring ideas is always inspirational.

Two people read this manuscript before it went to the publisher: Evan Cooper, who read it with a critical eye, and my husband, Gene Estess, who read it with an uncritical eye. Both were invaluable.

There are some people who contributed to this book without really knowing it: my parents, Adele and Milton Schiff, and four adult children, Andrea, Peter, and Jen Wohl and Noah Estess. I can't quite put my finger on the exact words of encouragement or assistance they gave me, but I felt their support with each word I wrote. Without them, this book wouldn't have been—couldn't have been—written.

Contents

Acknowledgments v

Chapter One
    In Pursuit of Trust 3

Chapter Two
    Talk to Me 19

Chapter Three
    Prenuptial Agreements:
    Terms of Endearment? 39

Chapter Four
    Your Home:
    Moving In, Moving Out, Moving On 63

Chapter Five
    ABCs of Money Management:
    Accounts, Budgets and Chores 81

Chapter Six
    When There's Not Enough 95

Chapter Seven
    The "Ours" Child 121

Chapter Eight
    Financial Links: They Extend from Former Spouse to
    Stepchildren ...and Beyond 133

Chapter Nine
    Remarrying After the Children Are Grown 159

Chapter Ten
    *Estate Planning: Assets, Heirlooms—and
    What About the Kids?* *183*
Chapter Eleven
    With This Checklist, I Thee Wed *215*
Chapter Twelve
    Conclusion *231*

Chapter One

In Pursuit of Trust

By the time you find yourself approaching or in the midst of a remarriage, you have packed considerable living under your belt. Your financial experiences—from childhood, single life, first marriage, divorce or death of your spouse, and single life again—form the basis of your opinions and attitudes about money. These beliefs become a way of life. Each person has a way of saving or not saving money, a favorite time of the month to write out checks, an entrenched view of how extensively to support the children's education, a feel for appropriate gift giving, opinions on vacations and investments, at least one irrational financial fear, and much more.

Priscilla had been married for six years to a semi-functional alcoholic who, as a chemical engineer, commanded a salary of between $60,000 and $75,000 when working. The income could have allowed them to live comfortably in Atlanta in the 1980s, but a third or more of each check was spent at bars and liquor stores or, occasionally, on repentant spending sprees that netted Priscilla roses and negligees, but no money for the mortgage. To insulate herself and her two young boys, Priscilla started stashing money from her salary in an envelope hidden in a book, vowing to use the cache for two things only: mortgage payments and the boys' education. When she divorced, she was stuck with $12,800 of her husband's credit card debt, which she started paying off slowly. Even then she didn't reveal the existence of her stash to creditors.

When she married Sy, Priscilla continued to tuck away dollars secretly whenever she could. One day, he happened on an envelope stuffed with more than $1,900.

Because each person brings his or her individual way of handling money to a remarriage, couples can't help butting up against each other when they remarry. No psychologist need tell you that if your actions are left undiscussed, resentment will build to the point that there's no trust left in the marriage. Most people who have been through divorce know lots about resentment.

"I was devastated when I found the money," Sy says of the envelope incident. "Of course, I knew about the financial hardships Priscilla had suffered during her first marriage and when she was raising the boys alone. I didn't care that she had this cache, but the fact that she didn't tell me about it indicated she didn't trust me. How could we live this way?"

Says Priscilla: " I had been so badly burned during my first marriage. My secret account was my carryover. But I'm glad Sy found the money. Although it caused terrible grief initially, the fights we had over it served as the basis for a new understanding.

"It took months for us to peel away and discuss all the fear I had—everything from being homeless to not having any control over my life—but as we discussed them, I felt better. Sy is really a wonderful person. He listened, he empathized, he shared with me stories in his life that were parallel or that revealed his own financial fears. And he did something I never could have expected, nor had I even thought about. He paid off the remaining $1,800 debt that I had inherited from my first husband. While he was writing out the check, I sat at the kitchen table and cried with joy and with love for him.

MONEY AND YOUR FORMER LIFE

Remarriages—by virtue of their "re" status—mean that something has gone wrong the first time. If your former spouse died, you might feel cautious, protective, or guilty for being happy. If you've gone through a divorce, you might bring a sense of distrust, guilt or illusion to this new relationship. Any of these emotions can affect your present finances. An adversarial attitude toward your former spouse in a divorce proceeding might spill over into the new marriage. Guilt over the breakup of a first marriage can lead to excessive generosity toward the first family to the financial detriment of the second. More subtle, but just as debilitating, may be the hope that this marriage will be everything the first was not, blinding you to the need to address practical financial concerns.

Because money has such powerful emotional overtones in a remarriage, and because there is no single type of remarried family (the variations are endless), there are no absolute or simple solutions. What's best is what you as a couple can agree on and that agreement takes time and talk.

Although it's nonsense to assume that if you talk about something before a remarriage you'll be able to work it out by the time the rings get slipped on, it is true that you and your partner can encourage the growth of trust by talking about obvious financial differences as soon as the relationship moves into a serious stage.

Before remarriage (and nonstop throughout it, of course), it's essential to be open and honest about your financial situation. Financial information—whether it's yours, mine, or ours—must always be shared. Putting down on paper the facts and figures of your assets, liabilities, income, expenditures and responsibilities is easier than discussing styles, attitudes and values. And just seeing those numbers on paper elicits a feeling of trust.

Numbers also serve as the basis for ongoing discussions. What lies behind them? While many of us secretly wish we were marrying for the first time (thus eliminating the former mates and alliances that are unfamiliar and wrenching to this new relationship), we realize that the soon-to-be-spouse is who he or she is because of the experiences that came before. Former husbands and wives are just that—former. And children from a former marriage are always children, even in cases where they are estranged. There is no such thing as an "ex" in a remarriage. You can't "ex" formers out of your life—like them or not. The Jewish proverb, "When two divorced people marry, four get into bed," survived because it's uncomfortably true. Whether through support or everyday existence, former spouses and their relatives constantly influence and intrude on the newly marred couple's lives—frequently financially.

The numbers prove it. "He still has to make payments on a Mercedes that his former wife's new husband drives," one irate second wife said about her executive husband, who was out of work due to a corporate merger.

Talking about the numbers uncovers more than a financial picture. It provides a mirror of who you are and what's happening inside of you.

Says one second husband, half-resentfully and half-admiringly, about his new wife's sense of loyalty: "There's $50 a month in our budget for her former husband's elderly aunt. She won't cut it out because this woman helped her out financially and emotionally during her divorce. It isn't much, of course, and it would be nice to use for dinner out occasionally, but...."

STAGES OF TRUST

Anita and Edward Metzen, who are remarried and researchers in the field, have defined five money stages most remarrieds go through.

1. The Rose-Colored Glasses Stage. In those romantic first moments, money talk seems crass or unimportant because the strength of love will handle everything (naivete) or there will be no money conflicts (ignorance).

2. The Don't-Rock-the-Boat Stage. Feelings of resentment or anger surface. Frequently such thoughts as, "Why should I resent his paying alimony? I knew about it before we got married," or, "I can't stand her

cheapness when it comes to gift-giving. I like to give the best," aren't voiced for fear that any stress would put too much pressure on the fragile new union.

In his first marriage, John had complete control over the finances. "I'm the type who, when I saw what I thought was a good investment, I borrowed money to take advantage of it," he said three years into his new marriage.

"I couldn't believe he would make these kinds of decisions without even speaking to me about it," said Judy, John's second wife. "But I hesitated to say anything because he wasn't signing my name to the loan."

3. The Lay-It-On-the-Table Stage. Couples painfully express their concerns to each other, feeling it's OK to be honest, to argue about spending priorities and to speak candidly about their feelings, frustrations and fears surrounding finances. A foundation of trust is being laid, albeit roughly.

   "I finally couldn't stand it anymore. After all, I was scrimping to contribute money into my 401(k) plan at work so we'd have money for retirement, and he was borrowing money for investments—which might or might not pay off," Judy said. "I told him I couldn't stand not being part of investment decisions."

   "I was surprised and more than a little annoyed at first," John admitted. "That's the way I've always operated. It was as if she didn't trust my judgment."

4. The Getting-It-Together Stage. The couple has arrived at a mutually agreed upon lifestyle and has established an effective method of handling finances and making financial decisions. This doesn't necessarily mean that they've commingled funds, just that they have agreed on contributions—both monetary contributions and contributions of time—and that they have a system in place for managing both jointly owned and separately owned property.

"Judy's a good money handler and I finally understand her need to be consulted before I make an investment, so that's how we handle this now," John said.

"But," Judy added, "we have separate accounts and John's debt and subsequent investments must be taken care of from his account. I don't try to dissuade him from the investment, unless I think it's a real rotten idea, because he's astute in this area. Though this type of money management still makes me uncomfortable, at least I don't have to see interest payments on a loan being written out each month."

5. The Achieving Stability Stage. The couple really reels in control of finances. Despite the ultimate instability of anyone's financial position, they now feel comfortable adjusting their goals or spending patterns, as circumstances require. Their perspectives are integrated. They can handle change.

"This year John had cancer surgery," Judy said, five years into the marriage. "For ease of managing money, we decided to join our accounts. We talk about everything now, but I'm handling all the money for a while. John trusts that I'll take care of things as best as I can. We're much more conservative now because, quite frankly, we don't know what the future holds."

ENTRENCHED MONEY STYLES

By the time individuals remarry, their culture, experience, personal chemistry and individual thinking have had time to mix and harden. They're fairly well-defined people who, as a couple, don't yet share a thick middle ground, defined as "an area of shared experience, shared values and easy cooperative functioning, created over time." This gives people a wide playing field for conflict. For a remarriage to work, the middle ground must broaden, according to Patricia L. Papernow, EdD., psychologist and noted expert in stepfamily matters.

Financial differences that turn on values, the principles that guide decisions, are the most difficult to resolve. Values stem from childhood and are expressed in political, religious and social orientation. Even without a conscious determination, they pilot people's actions as parents, spouses, employees and employers, community members, relatives and friends.

If two people have significantly different definitions of honesty, for example, they will have problems trusting one another. Suppose a husband is freewheeling with his expense account, charging everything—the family's sports event attendance, expensive dinners out, and much, much more—to the company, while his wife self-righteously seethes, about the abuse and refuses to go out with him if he continues. It's a bad sign for the marriage.

And there are even wider schisms. I know of one New York man who, in an effort to raise capital for a business, deliberately withheld information about his partners (two men who had served jail terms for grand larceny) from his wife's relatives when he asked them to invest in the deal. The projected profits, he reasoned, were more important than full disclosure. When his wife discovered the truth, she disagreed to strongly that, within a few months, she instituted divorce proceedings.

Clearly, remarrieds will not have identical value systems, but each of their highest priorities should be meshable if there's to be a possibility of planning and living a life together.

Values are different from style. Values are the conscious or unconscious beliefs you feel in your gut; style is the expressions of those values. You both might value financial security, but where one of you views it as owning your home mortgage-free, another might see it as having enough money saved or invested not to threaten your lifestyle if you decide to take a lower-paying job doing something you really love.

Style is influenced by many factors. Your personality and your confidence level are important ones. Introverts and extroverts might contribute the same $2,000 to the American Cancer Society each year, but one might do it anonymously and the other might want to be listed in all the charity's literature.

How you handle money also has to do with your confidence in your ability to earn it. One banker put it this way. "If I hadn't been let go twice in the past two years as a result of all these damn layoffs, I'd be a lot less skittish about dipping into our savings to buy a new car."

His wife, who is a nurse and never lacking for work, is much less concerned about the expenditure. "You'll get another job soon and you'll need the car. So why not buy it now since they're offering a good deal?" she argues.

People who make their first major foray into the workplace immediately after a divorce frequently feel and act as if they're one step away from poverty, even if they have substantial assets or earn an impressive salary. Their confidence as a moneymaker and manager has not yet developed. Often they drag that lack of confidence and its coexisting lifestyle into a new marriage.

Many marital arguments revolve around differences in styles. You know the scenarios. He never seems to worry about money; she comparison shops tomatoes. She constantly forgets to enter checks she writes in the checkbook; he's a fanatic about reconciling bank statements. He wants to give his children everything he didn't have as a child; she feels her children ought to be responsible for earning their spending money.

We were a screaming example of how the differences can affect a relationship. My husband, Gene, had a considerable support commitment and no savings. A year before we were married he returned to Wall Street after a two-year hiatus. It was going to take time to build up a client list again—we both knew that. In the first year of our marriage even our modest lifestyle meant we were living way beyond our joint incomes and deep into my limited savings. Our entertainment budget was confined to haunting flea markets on weekends and picking up old medicinal tins for Gene's collection. Though I loved the new activity, I lived in terror that

Gene would stumble on a "find" and plunk $200 down, pushing us still further into my savings. Initially, I'd balk at his purchases, commenting on "the condition" of the tin or finding some other reason why he shouldn't buy it. If he succumbed to my resistance, he'd sulk and insist on going home immediately. If he bought the tin, I'd pick a fight.

Do markedly different styles doom a remarriage to nagging, squabbles, resentments and down-and-dirty fights? No. Conflicts in style create problems because of the way they're handled, not because they exist. In their in-depth research on couple relationships published in *American Couples*, Drs. Philip Blumstein and Pepper Schwartz concluded that "the mere fact that a couple has very different ideas about how to spend money does not necessarily mean they have more conflict. If, however, [and this is especially important] in addition to having different view, at least one partner feels he or she cannot exert any control over spending, then we often observe anger and frustration."

Handled properly, different styles give the couple a new sense of closeness. They grow confident that they will be able to navigate other differences because they've reached a solution together.

While neither Gene nor I wanted to wind up in debt, for example, we had very different thresholds of comfort with our situation. Gene was confident he'd be financially successful again; I was wary and felt threatened. Eventually our accusations led to an expression of the real pressures each was feeling. Gene felt trapped in a financial half nelson. I was fearful we would further tip our already tilted financial situation. But we've always respected each other's feelings, so once we understood the fears and needs, we were able to work out a solution. We set a limit on our monthly flea market jaunts. We decided to buy some of the household items we needed at the markets—a bedspread, a lamp, and a spatula—so we could experience the fun of hunting even though we were shopping for necessities. And Gene suggested I start collecting the Depression glass water goblets I always admired. He was more than happy to suspend tin purchases to see the joy I got from buying one $5 to $8 glass each outing. It was a solution that worked for us.

Now, 25 years later, Gene and I exchange sly smiles when people comment on my wonderful goblet collection and his fabulous medicinal tins. They probably could never guess that those 28 glasses, costing maybe $250, saved us thousands of dollars on marriage counseling. And the goblet resolution was the first of many creative problem-solving exercises we have had to go through because of our different money styles. With each one, we've increased our closeness and our trust both in each other individually and as a team.

SPOUSES CAN ALTER STYLES

One spouse's distinct money style frequently has a definite effect on the other's. It can push people to the right or left of themselves.

Bob, a Boston entrepreneur, tells how his first wife spent money before he earned it. Nothing was too good for her or the children. The Tiffany diamond studs were a "must"; the children not going to summer camp was unheard of. He constantly found himself in the position of spoiler. "I was the one who told my daughter she couldn't have the diamond studs she wanted for her twelfth birthday. I was the one who screamed about department store bills as they came in each month. I didn't like being the ogre, but I always felt I had to balance my (former) wife's unbridled spending."

When Bob married Roberta, he took on a different persona—one of benefactor. He found himself prodding Roberta to buy a new dress or urging her to get the next-to-best room at a resort rather than the cheapest. "I'm now on the other end of the seesaw," he says.

"I have had to be very careful with money because I had so little when I was raising my children," says Roberta, who was a single parent for thirteen years. "I don't like to waste money. I don't care if it's Bob's or mine."

Bob claims he's much more comfortable in this new position, and Roberta says that even though she's still frugal, she's learning to loosen up and enjoy herself more. The shift in attitudes has not been dramatic, but it has occurred. And both feel better about it. Clearly people can relax and enjoy themselves more when they're neither too far left nor too far right of their gravitational middle.

FAIRNESS COUNTS...BUT NOT FOR EVERYTHING

Marriage is marriage, whether it's a first or second. Inherent in its meaning is financial fairness. To the extent fairness can be controlled, it should be, because it's a building block for trust.

Yet it's almost impossible to even out the ground. One of you might sell your house for five times its purchase price while the other barely breaks even. One of you might have been born to rich parents while the other was not. One of you might have stashed away $100,000 for a child's college education, while the parent of the child who's a far better student may have been saving nothing. Are any of these situations fair?

While we can try, eliminating the situations that foil fairness is like plucking weeks from the garden. You clear the area of choking growths, but you don't ensure flowering plants—or even that you'll be rid of weeds forever. Part of the problem is that you don't have ultimate control over financial fairness. So the question is, if establishing financial fairness is so difficult, is the struggle worth the effort?

In the end, the answer is equivocal. Certainly you should attempt to be fair. But where fairness isn't possible or sensible, work to find practical solutions and move on with life. Endeavoring to put fairness in terms of dollars and cents or participation, for example, may not be a productive way to build trust. You might have to find another way, such as accepting that there are certain financial situations that can't be balanced. If one of you has a $12,000 credit card debt, for example, it makes more financial sense to pay that off than to contribute an equal amount to the joint purchase of a new car.

MONEY TALK: AN APHRODISIAC

"Although it's more than 20 years ahead of us, we've been talking a lot about retirement recently," Derek said. *"I have fond memories of Oregon from when I worked there during one of my college summers. I've always thought that's where I'd like to retire. I thought it was important for Susie to see what I was dreaming of. She thought so, too. We really didn't have the money to vacation in style because I was paying my boys' college tuitions, but this past summer we used frequent-flyer tickets, took our daughter Christen (2), and stayed with my sister. It worked out fabulously. Susie fell in love with the land, too. Now there's something else we have in common, something we can look forward to and save for together."*

There's romance in dreaming together. A week in Martha's Vineyard, seeing a child graduate, or buying a home of your own are dreams that require planning—financial planning. Talks of an exciting future, like whispers of sweet nothings, have a way of heightening sexual closeness.

Remarried couples who don't use money talk to increase romance are missing out on the aphrodisiac of our time.

Money talk is good pillow talk, even when the intimacy achieved is not sexual. In times of financial crisis, people who have communicated their money values, attitudes and feelings are better able to support each other—emotionally and practically—than those who don't know each other as well. Quite simply, they trust each other more.

TRUST...AND A LEAP OF FAITH

Seasoned by care, communication, laughter, shared experience, effort, problems and problem-solving, a committed remarriage settles into a trusting relationship, one in which you feel safe. Your partner may not always handle money to your liking, but you don't feel like the actions are meant to harm you. Researchers say that it can take as many as seven years for this to occur, if you don't get mired in one of remarriage's developmental stages. Trust is built slowly, through a series of minor events, such as saving together to buy a home, giving a stepchild money for college, transferring a piece of property to a new spouse, or figuring out ways to merge financial styles. Most people don't have any idea when the trust has rooted. For others, the moment is seared in memory as an act of faith.

Cathy bought a three-year-old to this new union and Frank had a ten-year-old from a former marriage. "Three years into our marriage, Frank approached me with the idea that he'd like to adopt my daughter," Cathy said. (Her first husband had disappeared shortly after their baby was born, and when she was able to track him down, he was amenable to the idea of adoption.) "I'll never forget the scene in the lawyer's office just before Frank signed the papers. The lawyer said, 'Frank, I want you to understand you don't have to do this. More than that, understand that if your marriage to Cathy doesn't work out, you're financially responsible for this child. I'm going to leave you alone for a few minutes to think about that.'

"*Frank looked at me, looked at the lawyer, then said, 'I've thought about it. This is what I want.'*

"*I'd known for some time that I loved Frank. But from that moment on, I knew he was someone I could always count on,*" said Cathy, as a tear slid down her cheek.

Chapter Two

Talk to Me

"Whenever Laurie started talking about her concern that we didn't have enough money for this or that, I tighten up," says Greg, a forty-one-year-old Moline, Illinois, retailer. "It felt like a grade-B movie flashback to my former marriage, when all my first wife ever did was criticize me for not earning enough, for being a constant failure-no matter how hard I worked or how much I earned. So when Laurie voiced concern over money, it had a perverse effect on me. I just clammed up and wanted to go out and spend irresponsibly. Often I did. That just accelerated her panic, of course."

Says Laurie: "Since my motive in discussing money was not to belittle Greg in any way, but to plan as a couple how we should manage what we had, I didn't realize that I was evoking images of the 'queen of evil' or sounding like her, God forbid. Frankly, until he explained it—and that didn't come for maybe eight or ten months into the marriage—it annoyed the hell out of me that he wouldn't even talk about money matters and the he seemed to enjoy making me crazier about the subject than I already was."

Talk is a must.

Talking about money works on many levels. At different times in a relationship-at different times during the day-money talk can fuel conflict, can be the access route by which two people learn more about each other, or can be the stuff of dreams. Sometimes it can be all three at the same time.

Making allies of time and talk so they become planks of a wide middle ground of trust—the trust that serves as the basis for money agreement rather than conflict—is no simple task. It's difficult for a person who has been living alone and quite comfortable with independence; it's even more difficult for someone fresh out of a hostile divorce.

Major impediments of the free flow of a rational discussion are the subjects that provoke intense visceral reactions—your financial hot buttons.

HOT BUTTONS

Hot buttons flood people with anxiety triggered by feelings of insignificance, mistrust, anger jealousy, guilt, shame or sadness. The buttons themselves aren't universally dangerous. Consider some of the hot buttons encountered in a cross-country survey. Some may send sparks flying in you, too, but chances are most will leave you unmoved and wondering why they're cause for anyone's concern.

- *A single joint checking account.* "I don't want his alimony check written from our account. Why should I foot the bill for his mistake?"
- *Separate checking accounts.* "He loved his first wife more than he does me. He held everything jointly with her."
- *Former wife is going to Europe.* "That bitch. She doesn't stop suing me for more money and now she's off on a fancy vacation."
- *Former spouse's new wife is wealthy.* "He's living in a $800,000 home overlooking Lake Michigan. Why is he such a cheap bastard when it comes to out kids?"
- *His children go to camp.* "We're not going anywhere. His kids come before us."

- *Her daughter needs braces.* "It frosts me that her father, who's very well-off, won't pay for this because it isn't included in his separation agreement and I, her stepfather, will wind up footing the bill."
- *She pays for groceries, going out, the babysitter; he pays the mortgage.* "He always says that he 'keeps the roof over my head.' That's what me father kept threatening my mother with when she said she wanted a divorce."

DEFUSING HOT BUTTONS

Finding a way to defuse hot buttons is essential if you ever want productive talk on an explosive subject. One way, suggested by Linda Perlin Alperstein, a family therapist in San Francisco, is to open the conversation with a "time-setter": "You know, the subject of Johnny's braces has been on my mind. When would be a good time for us to talk about it?" Once you set a time, Alperstein says, you know your partner feels that it's OK to talk about this subject. Agreement to talk may be the only agreement you have at the moment, but at least it's a start.

Even more effective in cooling down hot tempers is what Alperstein calls the "If I Got You Correctly" excuse. "It's slow and it's tedious because it interferes with the way people normally fight. And it's hard work. But it is effective in defusing emotions and forcing people to listen to each other," she says.

It works this way.

1. You make a statement.
2. Before your partner can respond, he or she must rephrase what you said. "If I got you correctly, you are pissed off that you are being asked to foot the bill for Johnny's braces."
3. If the assessment is right, your partner proceeds with a response.
4. If the assessment is wrong (and only you can judge that), you have to rephrase what you said without going into a tirade).
5. If your partner assesses your feelings correctly, then it's his (or her) turn to respond.
6. You have to do a "If I got you correctly" rephrase of your partner's statement.
7. The process repeats itself.

"There are two key elements in the exercise." Alperstein explains. "The first is that you *don't have to agree, but you do have to understand* what your partner is saying. The second is that *understanding, by itself, can be a healer.* People don't have to be agreed with all the time, but they do need to be understood."

A CASE FOR "IF I GOT YOU CORRECTLY"

Knowing oneself doesn't assure change...or harmony. Consider June, a forty-nine-year-old woman from Rockville, Illinois, who cares for the home and her seventeen-year-old son (but not her husband John's children) and manages the couple's social life.

"My father died when I was seven. Thought my mother didn't have to be conservative with money, she was...and I felt very deprived. I've explored this

feeling of depravation at length with my therapist and I know that's why I married my first husband. He was very rich and would take care of me finan-cially. With John [her second husband of three months], I feel very loved. But I know myself. I wouldn't be happy with someone who doesn't have money. I need to be taken care of. I don't want to be poor."

June has made her position clear to John. "He knew before he married me how I felt, so he can't have complaints now."

But he does. "I understand June," John says, though he wouldn't discuss his feelings in front of her. "And I don't mind being the provider. I, too, was brought up feeling that that was my responsibility. But in my business (he's a real estate deal-maker), there's always the possibility that I'll have a really bad year. I'm having one right now. Even when June listens to me talk about busi-ness, I don't get the feeling she understands or wants to hear me. And it's not because she isn't capable. She's very capable. That hurts me. In addition to worrying that I might not be able to support her in the style we'd both like, I'm afraid she'll just take off and leave me the way my first wife did."

If "I got them correctly", June is panicked about the possibility of not having enough money, and neither she nor John is hearing the pain of abandonment each associates with money.

KNOWING THE FACTS

For the purposes of communication, knowledge of the actual (as opposed to the imagined) financial facts often can defuse the emotional flares asso-ciated with money.

John and June's money problems aren't severe. As John explained it, they have a reserve, upward of $500,000 in stock, and three pieces of property— their luxury condo and two rental properties that pay for themselves, though *they don't throw off much profit. His income has dropped, to be sure; it is down to $100,000 this year (compared to $250,000 for each of the past three years), but they certainly aren't starving. They don't really have to cut back on their expenses significantly, though it would make him feel better if they did. "The flower bills kill me. I know it's a small thing in the scheme of things, but I can't believe we spend $100 a week on flowers in the house. I've asked June not to do this anymore, but she insists—saying she's using her money, so why should I care. I wish she used her money for groceries when her son comes home from boarding school."*

If John were to lay out what they have, what they are bringing in and what they are spending, and if June could listen to John's recitation of the facts and be able to tolerate that he, too, needs time to worry, chances are she wouldn't feel so threatened when he complains about business. "I'm not going to fink out of my responsibility to support her," John says. "What I need is someone I can trust to complain to, to air my frustration with. I'm looking for a partner."

Sharing financial information is fundamental to a good marriage—even if it causes friction. The wife who gives her son $8,000 from her own account as a down payment for a car may be in for a "that-kid-doesn't-deserve-it" tirade from her husband, who doesn't share her largess. But the damage to the relationship from this conflict isn't as corrosive as it would be if her husband uncovered the secret gift later. It's not that the data itself is so important; the act of sharing confidentialities is what strengthens the bonds of love. Deep secrets between spouses can destroy marriages.

Whether before or during a remarriage, couples will feel more comfortable with finances if they share information about income, expenses and assets openly and regularly.

A "MORE TALK, LESS FIGHT" COMMUNICATIONS PLAN

"It sounds ridiculous, I know, but we have a regularly scheduled finance meeting on Sunday afternoon—after whatever major game of the season is being televised, naturally—and we talk about anything and everything dealing with our money," says Brenda, fifty-one, a high school social studies teacher in Miami, Florida. "In the early stages of our marriage, we talked about my anger over how much Milt gave his boys, and how unfair that was to my children; why I had a need to ask him before I bought anything, and how he resented that; our wills. Then, as our marriage rooted, we did more planning and less arguing. Now, sixteen years later, we are doing some estate planning, figuring out how to reduce taxes. Sometimes we just use this regularly scheduled finance time to write out checks."

Set a Specified Time and Place to Discuss Money Matters
The time should be convenient and the setting relaxed (not in bed, though, unless your talk is romantic—like planning a trip to Hawaii). Take a walk or sprawl out on the lawn if you have serious grievances to discuss. Use the dining room table if you need to spread out the checkbooks, budgets or investment statements—but sit on the same side of the table and not across from each other in a confrontational position. Don't pick a spot that weighs in someone's favor (like a room with one comfortable chair, not two) or anyplace where one of you feels insecure or out-of-place (like a study used by only one of you).

Set Ground Rules for Your Money Talks
Whether at scheduled times or spontaneous, money talks should focus on what you're feeling as well as the numbers. "I'm angry because your children get everything they ask for" is a more productive springboard for dis-

cussion and less threatening to your spouse than "Your children are spoiled brats." If one lapses into accusations, make it fair game for the other to ask for a rephrasing of the statement. And set a time limit on the conversation and don't allow it to drone on.

Because money is sometimes a cover for other issues, it's easy to go from one subject (like anger over having to use some of one's own earnings to pay for a stepchild's education) to another (being afraid you won't have enough money to finance the education of the child you had together). When you use one issue to delve into underlying concerns, that's productive. When you get sidetracked and jump from one money issue (car insurance) to another (gifts) in the same discussion, that's unproductive.

Base Your Talks on Facts
Having the facts in front of you diffuses the anxieties and often helps a couple find a solution to a money problem.

"I used to worry—and worry Suzanne—so much about finances, that we'd wind up screaming about it in some crazy frenzied state," said Noel, forty-two, manager of marketing support for an Illinois insurance company. "I was frantic about how I was going to put my three children and our two through college, about how we could afford to take a vacation, about how we were ever going to amass enough money to retire. Then, several years ago, I bought a $16 calculator that does present and future value analysis. It has done more for our marriage than any other purchase. I found out that even at an annual 5 percent inflation rate, we'd still have enough for retirement. Knowing that has helped relieve some of my pressure. We feel comfortable enough about our future that we took out a home equity loan to pay for my kids' schooling. Assuming we remain in good health, we'll be able to repay it easily in a few years. This calculator has brought a certain amount of peace to our lives."

Communicate Creatively

Realizing that each of you has different hot buttons, try not to aim for them. Seek an oblique approach instead.

Remarried couples have so many real issues to discuss, it may seem silly to drop everything to talk about a bunch of test questions posed in a book or magazine or to develop lists of spending priorities. But it's the very fact that these exercises aren't directly related to your life that makes them valuable and fun—and allows them to be used as the basis for creative financial planning.

Think, for example, of how you envision yourself financially five years from now, assuming there is no major collapse of the economy or your personal financial situation.

Ask yourself what money meant to your parents and to your former spouse. Was it meant to be saved, used for fun, for education, for the children or for giving to charity? How did these people's ideas about money influence your life? Sharing these visions and experiences helps explain who you are and why.

"I'm a very emotional arguer," says Ilana, a Los Angels mother of two toddlers. "I cry and become irrational. Then Paul says, in a very modulated tone, 'There's no reason to yell,' and it just gets me crazier. So I write him letters. They allow me to think through my anger and channel it into an explanation Paul will understand. When he comes home and there's a letter on his pillow, Paul knows there's something important we have to talk about."

If members of a debating team, professional salespeople, and super-articulate men and women practice how they're going to say something, why shouldn't you? Don't hesitate to practice in front of a mirror or write down opening lines.

Communicate Personally

Whatever the money concern, realize you're in a marriage together. Look at and talk directly to each other. Don't wait until your mother comes over to complain about your spouse's spending habits. Talking through another person is a trust-buster and rightly inflames emotions.

When looking at your finances and brainstorming for solutions, use "we" instead of "I" or "you". In a remarriage, each of you has added obligations—financial and emotional—but you're still a couple.   To   find out exactly where each of you stands and how far apart you are, you might give each other a chance to voice your "druthers."

He: "If I had my druthers, we'd track down Susie's father—no matter where he is—and sue him not only for back child support but for every other thing he said he's pay for that he never has."
She: "If I had my druthers, we'd forget he ever existed."

Anger with a former spouse has a way of spilling over into the current marriage. Fight the anger, not the new spouse. True, your first wife had an entitlement mentality that was infuriating and costly. But just because your present wife is excited about buying a new dress doesn't mean you have to tense up and start an argument—fearing a similar attitude. And if your first husband stalked around the house every hour shutting off lights in order to save on electricity costs, don't label your present husband cheap merely because he turns off lights when he leaves a room.

Don't Be Afraid to Disagree

As a married couple, you've created a safe place (institution, if you will) to fight about money—as long as you fight fairly. "The ideology of marriage helps a couple absorb a great deal without collapsing. Thus, permanence and security permit greater conflict among married couples," say Drs. Philip Blumstein and Pepper Schwartz in *American Couples.*

Realize There Are Some Gender Differences

Men and women traditionally feel and act differently about money. Money usually represents security and autonomy to women; to men it often means identity and power. To test whether you fall into the majority, discuss with each other what each of you means when you say "financial security."

Valuable communication gets lost because of cross-gender translation, according to Victoria Felton-Collins, author of the book *Couples and Money.* When men joke about money, women interpret it as not caring about them or the problem. When men advise, women think they are being patronized. When women confide a problem, men feel like they are being burdened with unnecessary information. When women confront, men interpret it as a nagging.

These are generalizations, of course. But examine your own discussions. Do they fall into these patterns?

Exacerbating the cultural and traditional money differences between the sexes are the differences in how men and women perceive the effects of their divorces. Women usually feel they were burned; men usually feel they were hung out to dry. While there are cases in which the man truly wound up the financial loser in a divorce, that isn't the general rule, statistically. In fact, on average, the standard of living for a woman with custody of children droops significantly after a divorce and a man's increases significantly.

Realize There Might Be One or Two Financial Areas Where You Feel There Can Be No Compromise, and Allow Your Spouse the Same Latitude

Everyone has some "musts' when it comes to money. And once the "musts" have been voiced, they must be respected (even if they're viewed as quirks or verging on insanity.). A "must" could be as simple as "I can't bear the idea of losing all our money in a bank failure; I want some within touching range." (In this case, you might have to stash some cash in the time-honored safe between the box spring and mattress) Or a "must" can be complex. "Because the cancer I had two years ago would be considered a preexisting medical condition when it comes to insurance coverage, I won't risk moving so far away that I couldn't work for this company any longer. Moving might jeopardize my coverage," said a Roanoke, Virginia woman contemplating remarriage to a Boston engineer. Her feelings are unequivocal; she would resent any attempt to talk her out of them.

Agree to Disagree or Postpone a Decision

There are money solutions that you can't (or don't want to) resolve in a session or a series of discussions. Sometimes you're too set in your ways; sometimes you don't trust enough. The passage of time can resolve conflicts, as can changes in the circumstances.

"I wanted him to take on some financial responsibility for my son's college education," Theresa said of her (third) husband, who had provided for his own children's education but wasn't anxious to be saddled with another tuition. "From the first week of our marriage, we battled. I insisted it was unfair that the children have different amounts available to them—especially because my son was a more diligent student. He felt it was my first husband's responsibility, even though the bum said he wouldn't do it. But since we were three years away from my son's freshman year, I backed off for a while." Eight

months later, Theresa's current father-in-law died and left her husband a small inheritance. "Even before the probate, Richard came to me and said, 'Don't worry about schooling. If his bastard father won't pony up, I'll pay for it.'"

Collaborate on a Settlement

Think of yourselves as partners in a head-to-head search for a fair agreement that will satisfy you both. Negotiating the settlement is a four-point process:

1. Separate the person from the problem. The problem isn't him or his children. The problem is that you feel jealous because he constantly gives his children gifts and you get nothing.

2. Focus on interests, not positions. Interests motivate us' they are the silent movers behind our positions. His position might be "I see my children so infrequently' I want to give them things." Your position is "We can't afford it." But if you allow each other to blow off steam and acknowledge and understand each other's emotions, then you can focus on what's behind the positions. Ask why. In this case, the interests—"It's important that my children feel loved" and "It's important that I feel loved"—are not necessarily in opposition.

   Then ask yourself what step you could take toward your partner's point of view. Even if it's a tiny step, such as, —"I'd like you to include me as the gift-giver once in a while"—it says you're agreeing to shift your position somewhat and concentrate on your partner's interest. He may respond with "Perhaps we can limit how much we'll spend when they come to visit." And so on toward a compromise.

3. Come up with a variety of possibilities before deciding what to do. There is never one right solution—especially in remarriages, where there are no textbook solutions. Try these techniques for brainstorming:
   * put yourself in your spouse's shoes
   * ask his or her advice on how to deal with the situation
   * adopt a no-criticism rule when a solution is offered
   * use one idea to generate another
   * dovetail differing interests

4. Base your decision on objective criteria. How much money is available is available for gift-giving—to children and to each other? What are other ways to show love? What have other couples done in a similar situation?

WHAT HAPPENS TO THE STUFF THAT DOESN'T GET SAID?

Fear of fighting, of uncovering sharp, irreconcilable differences, prevents some people form talking about what's on their minds. For example, Doris, a Detroit teacher, has no idea of whether or not her husband of five years has a will, and if he does, what's in it. "I'm afraid to ask him," she says. "What if he has left his children everything and me nothing? I'd be so hurt. And I don't know how to broach the subject. I don't like to talk of death, nor do I want to sound like I'm interested in his money."

Here is a communication gap that is eroding trust and could filter down to become a major financial problem. Even though under the laws of the state, Doris, as spouse, is protected from being disinherited, she doesn't know what she can expect, financially, if her husband dies. At this point, she'd do well to broach the subject not from the angle of wills and death, but by admitting to her husband that she's worried about not sharing something that has been on her mind.

When spouses refuse to address financial issues or pretend they don't exist, when they cloud financial issues or avoid dealing with the real issues, trust erodes—and with it the marriage.

Many people well-up with resentment over financial matters, but don't know themselves well enough to realize what's behind this feeling. Prodding feelings with "whys" and exploring background and experience together—either with or without the help of a professional—can break the communication logjam.

WHO CAN HELP?

Feeling nobody else has ever faced the problems of remarriage that you face is natural. Yet despite the uniqueness of your situation, there are identifiable patterns in remarriage. And talking to others about them is valuable because once you understand that you're not alone and that blame lies not with your spouse or the children, you can begin to address the complexities of remarriage. If your emotions are so close to the surface that you can't talk rationally to your spouse about them, seek help from people or groups who facilitate the art of talking to each other.

All over the country there are family therapists specializing in communication difficulties in remarriages and stepfamilies. Check with friends who might have had similar problems for recommendations.

The American Group Psychotherapy Association is a national organization, headquartered in New York City. It will refer you to therapists in you area specializing in remarital issues.

The Academy of Family Mediators, based in Eugene, Oregon, will send you a list of mediators in your area trained to help resolve all family disputes, whether they're support, custody, asset distribution or parent/child conflicts. Mediation has become a powerful tool in resolving family monetary problems because it forces you to talk to each other and to resolve your own differences.

The Stepfamily Association of America (SAA) is a national self-help group, headquartered in Lincoln, Nebraska, with local chapters in every major U.S. city. (For local chapter information, call 1-800-735-0329.) Its supportive comradery and vast collection of materials are valuable in helping remarrieds deal and heal. Laughter, tears, and a slew of good coping suggestions pepper the monthly meetings. Opening up to others helps you open up to each other. Listening to others helps you learn to listen to each other. The organization was founded in 1979 by two mental health professionals, John Visher, a psychiatrist and Emily Visher a psychologist. John and Emily are remarried themselves, and were very befuddled at fist by how to handle their new family. They decided to take an active approach, to become part of the solution and not part of the problem.

"I heard about the SAA about four years after we were married, and we went to a few meetings," relayed Peter, a systems analyst on Long Island. "I guess we were having some problems with my kids—even though they weren't living with us. The topic for one of the meetings was vacations and, boy, was I ready for this. It seemed to me we never saw each other anymore. Libby and I were both working long hours. We had just bought a house that was a wreck. When we weren't trying to fix it up, we were with my kids. I was drained of all energy—psychic and physical. I don't know what prompted me to open up and share these feelings with the group, but I did. I even told them I wanted to go to Mexico on a vacation. Libby hadn't known of that before this particular evening. She turned white, as if she was undergoing a spinal tap. We talked all the way home and long into the next morning."

"I had never realized the depth of Peter's need to go away before he mentioned it at the meeting," Libby said. "And I didn't really understand why I was so opposed to it. It was kind of a reflex reaction to growing up poor—we can't afford it, we can't take the time off now, that sort of thing. Our talking

forced me to look at the reality of the situation, which was that I had just got-ten a 20 percent raise [a move into management in city government] and that I, too, was exhausted. Surely we deserved this trip. We hadn't taken even a weekend to ourselves since our honeymoon.

"Still, I couldn't get myself to make the reservations. Peter had to do that. And to assure myself that I was worthy of the trip, I worked myself into a state of exhaustion the week before, staying at the office every night until eleven. I fell asleep on the way to the airport, woke up long enough to walk onto the plane, and then slept again for five hours. When we finally landed in Puerto Villarte, I looked around and couldn't thank Peter enough." Said Libby, "I'll always be grateful for that meeting, which forced Peter to talk and me to listen."

Comfort quotients differ when it comes to sharing thoughts, informa-tion and feelings. But for a couple to get through the better-or-worse, richer-or-poorer times, meaningful talk is essential.

Chapter Three

Prenuptial Agreements: Terms of Endearment?

Real people don't have prenuptial agreements. Or at least not most of the real middle-and upper-middle-class people I interviewed. Even if they were prime candidates for prenups—and there were many such people—a large percentage shied away from them. Interestingly, lawyers and financial planners—those very people who urge everyone with any assets whatsoever to "put something in writing" (The little "something" nets a nice fee) don't always heed their own advice. Randi and Roger Smith, a remarried Florida couple, meshed their personal and business lives five years ago when they became Smith & Smith, financial planners. Their rationale for not having an agreement, according to Roger: "We didn't need it. She came into the marriage with cash; I came in with the business. I accepted both the financial and time liabilities of her children."

"I don't tell people they *should* have one," said a Tucson financial planner, "just that they should consider it. We didn't have one. We have fairly equal assets and almost the same number of children. He has four; I have five."

So, what does this mean? Should we or shouldn't we be concerned about spelling out in advance of the remarriage how property we own is to be split in the event of divorce or death? Are we not as concerned about divorce (and its perilous negotiations leading to a division of property) as we should be? Is there too much emphasis on the subject of prenuptial agreements (also called antenuptial agreements), and too much pressure from financial advisors and friends to have them?

For most people the subject is moot—there's not enough in the way of assets to discuss. "That's something rich people can worry about, not us" is the typical response when a prenuptial is mentioned.

Others, still in the blush of romance, believe in each other. Right or wrong, they figure that the union will survive until death (when all that's needed is a will). In the unlikely event they do divorce, they feel that they will be able to work out an amicable way to divide property.

Some feel they are already protected, and they may be right. Most state laws provide spouses with limited financial protection, so in most cases they won't wind up penniless as a result of death or divorce.

And then there are people who might want to draw up a contract, but who are afraid to bring up the subject. They feel it's unromantic to plan a divorce at the same time they're planning a wedding. Or they don't want to cast themselves in an unfavorable light for fear "she'll think I don't trust her" or "he'll think I want to marry him only for his money."

Probably the only way to broach the subject in a way that will minimize resentment is to fame it in terms of trust (and to mean it). "I love you and have enough confidence in you and our relationship to raise tough and sensitive subjects, like a prenuptial agreement."

PRENUPTIALS ARE EXPLOSIVE

"I've never been part of a prenuptial that didn't generate some resentment," says on New York attorney, who claims to have drafted over 150, "even those done for all the right reasons and which are eminently fair by my standards."

Why?

There's a paradox inherent in a prenuptial. Says Mark Levinson, a Boston attorney: "By reducing a relationship to an agreement, you drain it. There's a realization that no agreement is worth the paper it's written on if someone decides to break it. All you have to do is look that Trump's well-publicized debacles."

Or perhaps by concentrating on financial matters surrounding death and divorce, you lose sight of a larger picture of love and commitment.

In cases where one is adamant about an agreement and the other less so, the process of drafting one sets resentment in motion. The tacit or voiced feeling: "If you loved me, you'd want me to have everything of yours, or at the very least access to everything—even though I don't want to touch it."

"Even when the person in the weaker financial picture tries to disavow his or her interest in the whole process," Levinson says of the scenario where one is pressing for the agreement, "as we go through it, tension builds."

"I represented the husband in an agreement he had never wanted." Says a New Mexico attorney. "He was a teacher; she was well-to-do—family money, high-paying job. After they were married, he became fanatic about keeping everything separate. He admitted that the reason was that he was angry with her for initiating the prenuptial. He felt vindictive and wanted her to live with the daily reminder that what was hers was hers and what was his was his."

Perhaps the most significant reason given by financial and psychological advisors who oppose prenuptials it that they are unrealistic. They give disproportionate significance to financial issues, then try to solve these issues in a telescoped period of time—the time it takes to draw up, negotiate and sign an agreement. Permanent financial resolutions can't be rushed by the deadline of a wedding, and temporary issues can change or evolve, these experts argue.

Prenuptials are temporary. Since it is impossible to anticipate events that will affect a marriage, prenuptials become outdated quickly. And the courts realize this. That's why, in recent years, the courts in many states are taking second looks at prenuptial agreements at the time of the divorce.

"Judges look to see if the prenuptial agreement was fair and reasonable at the time it was drawn up. But they also look to see if it is fair and reasonable at the time of the divorce," says Randy Kaplan, a Boston matrimonial attorney. "If it's a short-term marriage, the agreement will probably stand. If the couple has been married for ten years or more, it will probably be set aside."

To understand how circumstances change to negate the prenuptial naturally, consider this story:

"For months prior to our wedding we argued about a provision dealing with a sizable piece of property my husband owned," a Houston entrepreneur says. *"Two years later, that property had to be sold to pay off debts on his failing business. All the negotiating Ken and I did was for naught. What we were left with was enormous ill will, and now that has to be mended."*

So the question is: Is a prenuptial agreement a self-fulfilling prophecy leading to divorce or a breakup even before the marriage?

Some experts insist it is not—that the process of drawing up a prenuptial is prophylactic. "If the premarriage discussion of money ends in no marriage at all, I don't think of it as having obstructed a marriage," says New York matrimonial attorney Jacalyn F. Barnett. "I think of it as having prevented a divorce."

Others question the value of the agreements and postulate that there is a higher incidence of divorce among those with prenuptials than among those without them, because the people who want them reveal a lack of commitment right at the start of the marriage. Even if it were true, there might be other reasons for a future divorce among people signing prenuptial agreements. Resentment stemming from a feeling of being maneuvered into signing a prenuptial might be one; another might be that people who draw up prenuptials have more money that those who don't and can more easily afford to divorce.

IT'S THE PROCESS THAT COUNTS

Even if a prenuptial pact is not for everyone, the prenuptial process is. Talking about finances before the wedding widens the middle ground of trust that a couple needs for a successful marriage.

What should you be talking about—prenuptially?

The Financial Facts

Here's the essential financial information: what each of you is bringing to the marriage in the way of property (everything from assets to stock holdings), debts (from alimony and support payments to credit card balances), obligations (from support for parents to pledges to charities, and expected income (from every source). There are also other bits and pieces of information that complete the picture, such as how much life insurance you have and who the beneficiaries are, where you bank, what's in your safe-deposit box, and how much retirement savings you have. Even if you don't plan to have a prenuptial agreement, you should draw up a list of what you're each bringing into the marriage in the way of assets. Then date it and sign it. In the event of a divorce, this paper can be used to trace the ownership of assets.

What You Should Know About Each Other's Finances:

- Assets
- Income
- Financial history (if or when you ever had lots of money, if and when you were ever poor, what events moved you from one financial position to another, what events had a dramatic effect on the way you view money, etc)

- Legal and moral financial obligations (support payments, charitable commitments, etc)
- Expected future income (inheritance, pensions, retirement accounts, etc.)
- How much life insurance there is and who the beneficiaries are
- Heirloom objects owned
- The financial institutions (banks, brokerage firms, etc.) and people (lawyer, accountant, financial planner) who handle your money.

The Financial Considerations You Will Be Facing Immediately

Chances are you've had enough time together to know what financial challenges you face. Do your spending styles clash? Are you going to have to move to a bigger home or apartment because of the additional children who will be either living with you or coming to visit? Do you expect additional financial pressure from your former spouse? Is there going to be a significant decrease in household income when one of you loses alimony? These issues have to be addressed—and solutions sought.

What Each of You Would Be Entitled to by State Law in Case of Divorce or Death Without a Prenuptial Agreement

Nobody wants to think about divorce or death when entering a remarriage. But the possibilities for either exist and you need to play out the worst-case scenarios:

1. You're getting a divorce an you have to go to court and let a judge decide the terms of a separation agreement because you and your spouse can't negotiate one yourselves. (This is the least desirable alternative because of its emotional and financial toll, and because it rarely

offers creative solutions that would meet your particular needs.) In most equitable distribution states, if the courts have to decide who gets what in a divorce, you will both be asked to put all your assets on the proverbial table. Then anything that either of you owned prior to marriage is removed.

It used to be that anything either of you received during the time of the marriage, such as a gift, inheritance or bequest under a will, would also be removed. That's not automatically done anymore. "Inheritance, gifts and retirement funds that you have acquired during the marriage may be split," says attorney Randy Kaplan. "And that even includes inheritances yet to come." The courts usually take into consideration the length of the marriage and how much both parties relied on the assets during the marriage. Community property states—Arizona, California, Louisiana, Idaho, Nevada, New Mexico, Texas, Washington and Wisconsin—are the toughest in enforcing the equal division of assets in case of divorce.

2. One of you dies. Most state laws protect a spouse from being totally disinherited. States vary as to the minimum share of the deceased spouse's property a surviving spouse is entitled to—generally, it's one-third. In a few states, it's half.

Because state laws vary widely, it's important to ask an attorney what the divorce and inheritance laws are in your state and to talk about the impact they might have on you.

Drawing Up a Will

Being skittish about discussing death when you're beginning a new life is understandable, but not smart. Having a will is even more important in a subsequent marriage than a first marriage because your estate is so much more complex and because your wishes may be counter to how the state would dispose of your property if you died without a will (interstate). (Estate planning is discussed more fully in chapter ten).

The Subject of "Fairness"

One of the biggest thorns in a remarriage is the fact that the financial see-saw in not level. One of you is usually the financial "heavy" and the other in the "lightweight". That imbalance may never be shifted.

One person may be "giving up" an important asset for the remarriage. Consider Marjorie, a New York City woman who lives in a large, rent-controlled apartment. She is marrying Donald and moving into his home. What happens if the marriage doesn't work out and they divorce? She'll have to move out, and her housing costs will be many times what she had previously paid in rent. What's fair? Perhaps in recognition of her giving up her rent-controlled apartment, Marjorie should be made a joint owner of Donald's home. Perhaps a prenuptial agreement should provide for a substantial alimony payment if they divorce, one that would pay for an apartment comparable to the one Marjorie vacated.

The fairness issue creeps in before the wedding, in the early years of the remarriage, and even years later. "Her children get more money from their grandparents each year than I'll be able to give my children in a lifetime." "If I have to put up with his crass family all the time, why shouldn't I be entitled to half his inheritance?" "What's a fair amount to spend on enter-taining my children, who visit once a month, as opposed to her daughter, who lives with us?" "Our baby is entitled to more that his two teenagers."

A couple has to define fairness when it comes to the extended family. Is it equality? (As long as equality isn't measured in terms of "same," it might be fair. Giving all the children basketballs for their birthdays because the gift is the same isn't fair; giving each a gift her or she would enjoy that costs about the same as a basketball would be equal and fair).

Is it each according to need? (If one child's needs greatly exceeds another's—perhaps because of some psychological illness—should the biological parent assume all the financial costs for that child and still be expected to contribute half of his or her salary to the joint welfare of the new family? Will the other children be accorded an equal amount spent on them, even if they don't need it?)

Is it "yours is yours, mine is mine?" (How far can you play this definition out? Who will pay for wine the couple brings to a friend's home when invited for dinner if the friend was originally the wife's friend? What's fair if his teenage son eats three times as much as her four-year-old daughter?)

Is it determined on an incident-by-incident basis? (At different stages of their life together, a couple may have more or less money. What's fair at one stage may be unfair at another. Individual circumstances, too, are always in a state of flux. One person may lose a job; another may be forced to work part-time because of a health condition. Extended families are always affected by changes of fortunes, so what's "fair" for them changes frequently.)

Your Goals and How You'll Finance Them

You've probably shared dreams; they may even be part of the bond you have with one another. They could include having children, buying a second home by the seashore, starting your own business, changing careers or retiring on a forty-acre farm. Whatever they are, you need a plan to finance them.

PRIME CANDIDATES FOR PRENUPTIALS

We attended a wedding recently where both he and she were remarrying; he for the fourth time, she for the third. The minister is asking them to repeat some very traditional vows, I thought. The last one they exchanged was "With all my worldly goods, I thee endow." On both sides of the aisle, the bride's and groom's, there was an audible gulp and then some whispering. All the invited guests knew the financial trials and tribulations at least one of them had gone through during a previous divorce. But we weren't sure the minister had the same information. And we all wondered, some silently and some more brazenly later, if they were indeed joining all their finances.

WHAT MAKES A FAIR AGREEMENT?

* *It protects and comforts both of you.* For the contract to be a stepping-stone to a committed relationship, it has to be created in a spirit that's caring and protective of each other.
* *There is full and fair disclosure of what each of your individual assets and financial liabilities are.* That's hard for some people.

Says a matrimonial attorney in Atlanta: "I have found that one of the most pervasive secrets men have is how much support and alimony they have to pay. When male clients come in to discuss a prenuptial agreement and I tell them they have to reveal their alimony and support obligations, about 10 percent walk out and never return. The issue of how much they pay seems to be an embarrassment." The attorney, a woman, says that women, on the other hand, generally want their future spouses to know how considerable their support from a former husband is, "so the new husband can appreciate how much alimony they're giving up for this union."

*You enter the agreement voluntarily. If at any time you feel your new mate is holding your feet to the fire because of mortification, financial devastation, or the betrayal he or she experienced in a prior relationship ("I want to make sure you don't do to me what Betty did") or you're feeling coerced into making concessions ("I'll call the wedding off unless you sign"), back away and review the situation. You shouldn't be punished for someone else's sins. Nor should you be threatened into signing. In line with that, the agreement should be signed by both of you as far in advance of the wedding date as possible (at least one month) or else it feels like a shakedown (and might be interpreted as such if challenged later on).

*You understand the provisions in the agreement and their potential ramifications. For your own safety, and to make certain the agreement holds up in the event of a later challenge, both of you need separate legal representation. No matter how comfortable you feel with the attorney who's drawing up the agreement, hire another lawyer to review it to protect your interests. If one of you is very well-off and the other would find it an economic hardship to retain a lawyer, the wealthier person should offer to pay for other's counsel, but the payer shouldn't have any say in the choice of the independent counsel selected by the other person.

Consider a Prenuptial Contract if...

- *You are remarrying later in life.* When the couple has built up a sizable estate and there are adult children, a prenuptial agreement makes sense.

- *You or your spouse is giving up something substantial in order to enter this marriage.* A woman gives up her career to bring up his children. A man postpones retirement so that he will be in a better position to help support his new wife and her children. A prenuptial agreement may be helpful in these situations.

- *You and your spouse want a prenuptial agreement.* Two extremely independent, financially successful people may want something in writing before getting married. Sometimes they feel they had to give up too much in a prior divorce, and therefore are very protective about assets.

Sometimes they want to guard their financial autonomy because they have invested so much of themselves in developing it.

- *You or your spouse (or both of you) is an entrepreneur.* Nobody benefits when the long-term success of a business is threatened by divorce or death. The entrepreneur might want to separate the business form other marital property and make independent provisions for its success and survival.

- *One spouse doesn't have complete faith in the other.* This is not to say that trust won't develop—in time. It's just that it's not there now. (Under the best of circumstances, people shouldn't marry until they feel more comfortable with one another. But that's not always the reality.)

WHAT TO THINK ABOUT BEFORE SEEING AN ATTORNEY

Since the purpose of a prenuptial agreement is to spell out how to split the property you hold individually and jointly in case of a divorce or death, you should think about how you'd handle the following elements…and the consequences of you actions.

* *Property you brought to the marriage.* In most cases, you'll want to retain sole ownership of these properties. In cases where one person owns everything going into the marriage, he or she may want to consider transferring some assets to the other person a bit at a time. If real prop-

erty is transferred, it must be conveyed in a legal fashion, including recording the transaction with governmental authorities. Consider transferring the property after the marriage to avoid taxes. (Married couples can transfer assets to one another without incurring any gift tax.)

In some states, if one or both of you is bringing property into this marriage that you intend to keep as yours (such as a country home or shares of stock) and want to make certain the income from these assets remains yours as well, all you have to do is sign a unilateral statement that says the income from this individual property shall henceforth be individual and not marital. The statement must be notarized and given to your spouse within a certain number of days after signing it. The nice thing about this is that if that's all you're concerned about, you don't need a full-blown prenuptial agreement.

* *Property obtained during the marriage.* In most states, property obtained during the marriage will be considered jointly owned when it's divided during a divorce, unless it can be proven otherwise.

* *The increase in value of property you own separately during the time of the marriage.* Suppose the property is improved, or taxes or upkeep are paid out of money in a joint account; how should the increase in value be assessed? For instance, suppose each spouse has 100 shares of a different blue chop stock when they enter the marriage. They divorce four years later; one stock has quadrupled in value and the other is worthless because the company went bankrupt. What happens now?

* *Pension and employee benefits and insurance.* Who are the beneficiaries? Are they determined by a separation agreement from a prior marriage? Will the new spouse be sufficiently protected in case of death?

* *Pre-existing debts and liabilities.* When a person has debts to repay, it means that, by definition, less goes into the marital pool. Should there be recognition of the fact that one partner is using marital assets to pay off premarital debts? Should the other spouse be compensated for this?
* *Compensation for someone who is making a financial sacrifice.* Will there be a transfer of home ownership into joint names, for example, if the woman suspends her career to stay home to care for his children?
* *Support for children from previous marriages.* Will he pay for her children's college tuitions the same way he pays them for his children? Some stepparents with enough money and good relations with stepchildren do offer to pay part of all of the children's tuitions. Others either don't have the money to fund all the education or don't see it as their responsibility. Some offer to help with repayment of student loans; usually that's at a later date, when their relationships with stepchildren have normalized and a bond between them has developed.
* *Support and division of property in case of divorce.* This is the fail-safe provision—the negotiation of a separation agreement prior to the actual even. In the case of support, there are generally three ways of handling it: complete waiver of support rights, a lump-sum payment, or periodic payments.
* *How the terms for rights to your estate or property might vary depending on factors such as the length of the marriage or birth of children.* For example, a couple might agree that the wife is entitled to 5 percent of her husband's premarital assets for each year of marriage—to a maximum of 50 percent. So in five years, she'd be entitled to 25 percent; in ten years, 50 percent.

Forget about including any mention of who's going to care for the children, do the house work or take the cat to the vet's, the religion in which you're going to raise the children, or any other lifestyle matters. Most courts won't enforce these clauses, though their inclusion rarely invalidates the prenuptial agreement's other provisions.

The courts are especially protective of children. Their support and well-being cannot be threatened by either parent's signing a prenuptial agreement. Nor can you preordain what's to happen to them. "A prenuptial agreement I refused to do involved a man marrying a woman with a child from a former marriage. He wanted an agreement that said if they had a child and the marriage dissolved, he would get this child—since she already had one," said one New York attorney. "If they had two children, he wanted his choice of child. And if there were three, he'd get two of them. Basically, he wanted the pick of the litter. I heard later that they didn't get married."

WHO SHOULD DRAW IT UP

You can draw up a simple agreement which says, basically, "Here's what each of us owns today, and what's mine will be mine if the marriage dissolves. Anything we acquire during marriage will be split 50-50." Attach the document to a schedule of possessions, have it notarized, and you have an executed prenuptial agreement that most courts will uphold. For an added measure of safety, ask a lawyer to review it and give an opinion as to whether or not it will stand up in court. But don't be talked into an extensive document—unless, of course, you feel you need it.

Use a matrimonial lawyer if you are not a do-it-yourselfer or if your assets are entangled, complex or numerous. Most are experienced at drawing up prenuptials and adept at running their clients through the prenuptial "what-ifs."

"It's interesting that even though people may have decided to go ahead with a prenuptial, they come to my office not wanting to bring up their private agendas," Boston attorney Mark Levinson said. "They look to me to speak the unspeakable. So I do. I say, 'Let's take some absurd scenarios. You get married Friday night and on Saturday one of you takes off. How would you want your finances divided then?' From there it becomes easier to discuss other scenarios."

Depending on the complexity of the agreement and the address of the law firm that designs it (Park Avenue firms in New York have greater overhead that Main Street firms in Tennessee), legal fees for the drafting attorney will run from $500 to several thousand dollars. Be certain to have a complete understanding in advance of what the fee arrangements will be. Most lawyers will require a retainer (an upfront payment). Insist on a letter of agreement from the attorney outlining the amount of the retainer and the scope of what it covers, the hourly rate of each attorney who will work on the matter, a statement that the retainer represents an advance against the time actually spent on the matter, and who will be responsible for expenses and what the lawyer means by expenses (you may be asked to pick up photocopying charges or the attorney's lunch bills if he works through lunch!).

Scale down the number of hours your attorney will have to put into this project by doing some preliminary work, like putting your financial records in order.

And remember: Each of you should be represented by your own attorney.

WHEN, WHY AND HOW TO AMEND OR NEGATE A PRENUPTIAL

As a marriage matures and as life changes, so must a prenuptial agreement. It's necessary to initiate periodic updates based on:

- events (you have a child together, one of you gets seriously ill, one of your parents becomes financially dependent on you)
- the number of years married (you will have a very different relationship ten years after you sign the agreement)
- a shift in tax, estate or marital laws

Whether an agreement is amended or negated, it can't be done unilaterally. Both of you must agree in writing to changes. And both of you should sign the additions or a statement of dissolution before a Notary Public.

You can negate an agreement three ways: Destroy the original and all the copies of it; draw an *X* through it (and all copies), write "No longer valid," and initial and date every page; or draw up a statement which says you both have agreed to negate the agreement, then sign it in front of a Notary Public.

ANOTOMY OF A PRENUPTIAL—IN STAGES

For Tandy and Robert the prenuptial agreement they signed just two weeks before their marriage was really the third version of an agreement they had drafted two years earlier when they moved in together and, without lawyers, negotiated a cohabitation agreement. You would think that after this cohabitation agreement and an engagement agreement, the prenuptial would have been a snap. It wasn't. "Those final negotiations were wrenching," said Robert. His ambivalence about the process was evident when he said, "No one can convince me it's like a partnership agreement. In business you provide for the success of a partnership in addition to what happens in a split-up. But the sole purpose of a prenuptial is what to do in case of dissolution. There is nothing positive in that. Yet I probably would go through it again. The agreement was important to both of us."

The facts: *Tandy is in her late thirties, divorced, with custody of one daughter, age nine. A couple of years prior to her divorce five years ago, she founded a service business in Detroit. The business has done nicely—not sensationally, but it's on the verge of franchising.*

Robert is in his mid-forties and has two children—one a freshman in college, the other a freshman in high school. He was divorced six years ago. Recently Robert sold an eminently successful business and realized an enormous profit. By his own estimation, "I'm very sound financially...and cash flush."

Agreement One

"I didn't realize what an emotional and financial commitment it was going to be when we moved in together," Tandy says. "First, I rented out my small house and he bought a large one—big enough for us, my daughter and his visiting teenagers. That meant if we broke up, I'd have to find another place to live— I couldn't kick the renter out—and my daughter would have to change school districts. I started to have flashbacks of what happened in my first marriage, when I got creamed financially and *emotionally. I felt a cohabitation agreement would help me deal with the anxiety. I needed to have in writing that in case we wanted to separate, Robert would come to at least two months of therapy with me so that I could fully understand the reasons behind the split. My former husband didn't. He was here one day, gone the next—to another woman. And because I didn't want to experience the same frightening feeling of being penniless that I had before, I wanted Robert to assure me of some money to rent a place in the same school district and to see my daughter and me through any therapy we needed."*

"Although I didn't mind the discussion, I was offended by the cohabitation agreement," Robert says. : *I felt, 'we have this wonderful life together, why would you want to screw it up with a signed document?' I knew I would help Tandy financially if we were to break up."*

The discussions were bruising—so much so that they sought the help of a family therapist, and then a psychologist. They dug for the underlying reasons for their attitudes.

"Robert is a wonderful, open man, ready to listen to my concerns, even though he might not understand or agree with them," Tandy says.

"I wasn't used to discussing financial issues with my mate—I've always made the decisions—and had to learn the process." Robert says.

Agreement Two

At about the time an engagement ring was slipped onto Tandy's finger, the couple decided to draw up a second agreement. It was constructed as an add-on to the cohabitation agreement. Whoever left the house would have to sell his or her share to the other person (as if Tandy were joint owner). Since Tandy didn't have the money she would need to do that if Robert left, Robert established an account for her for just that purpose. Robert also took out an insurance policy naming Tandy as beneficiary. Each drew up a new will, naming each other as executor, but sill leaving their respective estates to their children. Again, the contract was self-drawn and self-executed.

Agreement Three

The prenuptial. *"We thought we could do this ourselves, too,"* Robert says. *"We couldn't. First of all, we didn't know what the state laws were and if we were violating them. For example, we had a sexual fidelity clause in it initially where we agreed to give up to 50 percent of any marital property if we violated that clause. This, the lawyers told us, was too punitive and wouldn't stand up in court. Also, we were dealing with more—and more complex—issues. The inequality of what we're bringing in to the marriage, for one. And that's always been a source of conflict. We went as far as we could go in our own negotiations and then said. 'Let your attorney talk to mine.'"*

Tandy says: *"Robert's financial success in business is shielded from me because it came before we were married. But mine will probably happen during our marriage. Does that mean I should share equally everything I've struggled to build simply because he married me at a better time? That wouldn't be fair. So we've made some compromises. The growth in my business will not be considered marital property; the appreciation on a piece of property he owns won't either.*

"If our reasons for having a prenuptial weren't so valid." Tandy says, two months after the wedding, "I don't think we would have survived the process. But the agreement will last because it was drawn up in a spirit of fairness, love and respect and built on a foundation of openness and trust. It has helped us solidify our emotional commitment and delineate the balance of power. And we've almost *learned how to resolve conflict."*

ONE MORE BUILDING BLOCK

Whether or not you have a prenuptial agreement, you must flush out your immediate financial concerns (which are almost always entwined with emotional ones). For most people, the prenuptial *process* will be enough, especially if you maintain mutual respect and a sense of fairness during the discussions.

If, indeed, you're candidates for a prenuptial agreement, tackle the process logically. First, understand the emotional reasons behind your position and your prospective spouse's. Second, go about the business of drawing up a prenuptial in a businesslike manner. Third, come up with a document that both of you consider fair. If you are looking for a committed relationship, consider the prenuptial as terms of endearment.

Success builds on itself. The better you can address today's problems, the more triumphant you will be in meeting other financial issues faced over the course of a marriage.

Chapter Four

Your Home: Moving In, Moving Out, Moving On

Often the first order of financial business a remarried couple must address is where to live. Home for remarrieds is not only where they hang their proverbial hats. It may be where your wife's former husband also hung his chapeau. It may be where your husband's first wife conceived their children and cooked their dinner. It may be your new spouse's bachelor apartment or the place you've been raising your children as a single parent. It maybe space new to both of you.

None of these choices might be to your liking. You may feel like an intruder, a person living with someone else's history, a stranger in an uncomfortable house or a transplant. Merging households means that as a couple you're saving money-but merging is always difficult, whether it's done someplace new or in a place where one of you has been living. Yet there's an air of excitement, of adventure, about it. There is no universally "right" place to live when you remarry. Whether you're moving in or moving out, it's important to move on and develop your own identity as a couple in a home that reflects the two of you.

A HOME OF YOUR OWN

"I'll never feel comfortable in this house," Marty says. The house is a colonial that Darlene bought when she was married to her first husband, a house she and her son had living in for four-and-a-half years before Marty moved in.

"Even if Darlene consults with me on changes, I feel it's hers. I don't feel entitled to make decisions. Something as simple as which wallpaper we hang in the bathroom doesn't seem like my domain. I prune the hedges with trepidation. I'd trim them down to a fraction of their present height, but I hesitate to take liberties with her property. I can't wait until we can afford to sell this house and buy one that's ours."

Most couples want to write the first chapter of their new marriage in a home neither has lived in before. If you can afford it and there are no mitigating factors, such as the need for you or a family member to be near a special school, doctor or instructor, or a separation agreement that prohibits the move until a child is of a certain age, then, from a psychological standpoint, neutral space is a good way to start life together.

Not that it's easy. Husband, wife and all the children living with you will feel a little shaky on this new foundation. That can be positive. You're sharing an emotion and an experience: anxiety in your new surroundings.

"I didn't anticipate that the move across town would be a big deal," says Jane, a human resource manager for a large New York company. "But it was. My daughter had to change elementary schools, which meant she had to establish new friendships: She was bitter about that. My husband Chuck found the commute into the city longer and more annoying than when he lived in a condo right off the highway. And I hated the neighbors. One had a tea to introduce me to the women on the street soon after we moved in. It was awful. I was put on review; they were brazen with their questions. 'Had I lived with Chuck before we bought this house?' 'Was he the reason for my divorce or was I the reason for his?' 'Did we plan on having children of our own?' I remember coming home afterwards and crying bitterly, certain we had made a mistake moving away from areas that we knew.

"It has worked out," reports Jane, three years after the move. "When my daughter went to middle school, she felt like a queen bee. She knew just about everyone—the kids from her old elementary school and those from her new

one. Chuck has adapted to the longer car ride and likes having a house to put-ter in. And I've become friendly—not friends—with these suburban home-makers who never before had known a remarried woman."

Make no mistake about it, however, a home of your own is not neces-sarily a panacea. Ellen, an Atlanta psychotherapist, didn't find the new house curative.

"Before I was remarried, I owned a home bought with the $30,000 inher-itance I received from my parents. It was just big enough for me and my two girls. I was proud of it; it was my symbolic and real financial security. When I remarried, I sold it and used the profits for a down payment on the large home Dale and I jointly owned. Years later, I realized that I had resented doing this. The first reason was the $30,000—which had grown to $75,000 by the time I sold the small house—represented something like a birthright to me, espe-cially since I'd grown up in a poor family. I didn't want to share it. And second was that, even though Dale was paying for the upkeep, this new house was much more costly to maintain. I worried that if Dale and I were to split up, I wouldn't be able to afford it. I felt at risk. What I didn't realize then, but do now, was that my investment in the small house represented my personal strug-gle for identity."

Ellen and Dale's unique resolution: Dale returned Ellen's down pay-ment to her. With that money, she bought a condominium that she does with as she pleases. At different times she has rented it out or allowed her two college-age daughters to live there rent-free. Once, during an eight-month separation from
Dale, she lived there. Dale owns the house. They have informally agreed that should they separate the house will be his—though he has willed it to Ellen should he die before she does.

SELLING YOUR OLD PLACE

Most people can't afford to buy another house before their first one is sold (or at least don't feel financially comfortable with the idea). So in the case of a remarriage, it might mean waiting until both of you go to contract on your respective homes before you seriously make offers for one of your own (although you should have been looking all the while). In tight real estate markets, this could take a year or more. Then there's another consideration: One or both of you might own a home with a former spouse who, according to a separation or divorce agreement, has to be consulted on and agree to any sale of that property. If the spouse resents the new marriage or wants to nettle you, he or she might arbitrarily claim the price being offered is too low and try to thwart the sale. In that case, you'll have to follow the procedures to settle the dispute outlined in your agreement.

If you want to sell quickly, you must be willing to sell at a fair price. A reasonable price (determined by appraisals from three or four brokers plus checking the recent selling prices of comparable area homes) will draw more buyers than a high one tagged "negotiable." And dropping the price of the house below a benchmark figure like $200,000 often helps.

Consider an auction if selling quickly is important. About 5 percent of all houses now are sold through auctions—a sales technique that is used more frequently when the economy and especially the real estate market, falters. The best way not to take a beating at auction is to set a minimum reserve price on your home. If bidders don't meet or exceed it, there's no sale.

What if, in a rush of enthusiasm, you buy a house together before either (or both) of you has sold the old house because you didn't need the cash from the sale of on to buy another?

In slow markets, when sellers squirm and buyers become ferocious bargainers, you might consider renting the house for a while. It means you'll have to postpone selling—which could be a blessing if the real estate market shows signs of coming to life soon. If you rent the house furnished, it provides you with storage opportunities for some of the duplicate pieces of furniture you probably are bringing to this marriage. And renting a furnished home or condo on a short-term basis is attractive to many people who are just moving to a locale.

The best renter is a prospective buyer who will lease your home with an option to buy. This agreement allows the lessee to apply some portion of the rent toward a purchase, say at the end of a year. The arrangement can be structured to make the future purchase more appealing; for example, by assigning 50 percent of the monthly rent toward the down payment. The renter then has to contemplate how much money is lost if he or she walks away without buying at the end of the rental period.

Keep the tax rules in mind. You don't have to live in the house to take advantage of the tax deferment given to those who sell a principal residence and acquire another at the same or a higher price within two years, buy you do have to prove to the IRS that you're renting as a stopgap measure, that the rental was meant to be brief. And during the time of the rental you can still deduct mortgage interest and property tax—though, of course, you must claim the rent as income.

BUYING A HOME TOGETHER

Whether it's a rented apartment in the gatehouse of an estate or the estate itself, a home represents a haven. Even more than what we wear, it reflects our personalities, our interests, our attitudes, our needs, our tastes and the state of our finances.

Normal differences, such as whether you want to climb stairs, live in a socioeconomically homogeneous neighborhood, feel uncomfortable if your neighbor's kitchen window is ten feet from yours, or prefer a Tudor or split-level, must be resolved when two people decide to buy a home together. A remarried couple has the following additional considerations.

- Where will you buy? In the community where the children living with you are going to school? Close to noncustodial children so you can see them frequently? Near supportive relatives or friends? In a community where one of you lived before? Far from a former spouse?
- Who is responsible for the down payment and the mortgage? This becomes a particularly thorny problem when one spouse has considerably more money than the other.
- What's the best way for the house to be titled, taking into consideration estate plans and the possibility of divorce?
- Are you planning to have children of your own? If the answer is "yes" should you buy a place you can grow into?
- Can you afford and do you want to provide bedrooms for children who visit? Whether you have a "child-in-every-bedroom" home or not, you'll want to provide visiting children with comfortable space of their own (no matter how small) so they don't feel they're intruding when they sleep over.

WHO OWNS THE HOUSE...EMOTIONALLY?

Larry and Miriam are engaged. But the question of home ownership has become such a thorn that unless they can resolve it, they probably will not get married. Larry, a New York City architect who hasn't been married before, has a net worth of $350,000. That's about fifty times his fiancée's net worth. "I never thought of the difference in our assets or our earnings until we began to talk about buying a house. Miriam, a social worker who has been supporting her two children, each form a different marriage, couldn't contribute to the *down payment on our $275,000 house. I knew that. But I didn't think she would expect equal ownership. She does. And I have mixed feelings about that," Larry admits.*

Legally, in most equitable distribution states, property *might* by considered separate during a divorce action if one spouse buys the house before marriage with money he or she had before the marriage, never transfers the title to joint ownership, and maintains the house as a separate property during the marriage by paying for everything connected with it—mortgage, utilities, repairs or additions—for the entire time the couple lives in the house. At that time, if they can't negotiate a settlement, a court will usually balance separate ownership with what it considers fair in these circumstances. In Larry and Miriam's case, it might take into consideration Larry's intent when he purchased the house, why he wanted separate ownership, Miriam's expectations, how long they lived there together as husband and wife, their needs and their other assets. In community property states, "fair" isn't considered. In those states, virtually all assets that a couple owns or develops together during a marriage are automatically deemed the property of both. So if Larry and Miriam lived in a community property state and if Miriam were to pay the mortgage a few times or pay for a new roof, the courts would say she had a half interest in the house because she had been part of its development.

The only way to ensure that the house remains separate is to draw up a pre-or postnuptial agreement which both parties willingly sign.

Is "separate" the best way to own a home, though?

Not necessarily.

Mention "home" and people think of roots, permanence, commitment, financial security and stability—all compelling feelings for married couples. That's why "home ownership" figures so prominently in the minds of people—especially people who have been hurt or disappointed in a prior marriage. So when one spouse "owns" the home, it's as if he or she has a lock on roots, security and permanence, while the other spouse is shut out of them. It's psychologically unequal. The non-owning spouse might justly wonder, "Why even bother about buying a new place to life? Why not just move into your present abode? It would make me feel just as uneasy, insecure and financially at sea a s living in a new house that I don't have an ownership interest in."

Larry's resistance to buying the house jointly reflects a tentative commitment to the relationship. He wants roots and security, he says, "but never having shared a life with anyone before, I'm plenty scared. I keep thinking that when I sign a check for $55,000 for the down payment, it's like I'm giving Miriam a $27,5000 gift—even before we're married. And then, though I don't expect her to contribute much to the upkeep of the house, if we were to separate, she'd get half of it. That doesn't seem fair to me."

Miriam admits her desire for ownership is also rooted in skittishness about the marriage. "My track record for marriages isn't great," she says. "I've made two mistakes—bad ones. While I don't think Larry is anything like my other two husbands, I'm unsure and trying to protect myself and my children—at least financially."

One workable solution would be for Miriam to contribute toward the down payment. A real stake in this house would serve to minimize Larry's control *and* his resentment. Even $2,000 (of her $7,000 savings) to Larry's $53,000 would go a long way; it says, "I'm willing to take a financial risk on this because I love you and trust in our future." For Larry to understand the depth of the commitment, he'd have to do some math: Miriam's $2,000 represents about 30 percent of her savings; his $53,000 is 15 percent of his.

TAKING TITLE: WHOSE NAME SHOULD THE PROPERTY BE IN?

As we have just said, title is less important in divorce than in death. Many states assume that a married couple's contribution to a home they live in is equal, no matter whose name is on the deed. Thus, in a divorce the property is usually split equally, unless some other division seems more fair or equitable, or an agreement can be reached by the spouses outside the court's domain.

For remarried couples, *how* the house is owned is far more pressing at the time of one of their deaths—especially if one or both spouses want to leave some of all of their share of the home to a child from a former marriage.

Usually a couple buys a home jointly as *joint tenants* with a right of survivorship. That means when one dies, the other automatically becomes the sole owner. Holding title this way is best for remarrying couples with no or young children. It also works well for couples who want their spouses to have sole ownership when one dies, so that the survivor can continue living in the home without interference or sell it and use the profits to maintain a lifestyle.

Holding a home as joint tenant's means that one spouse can insist upon the sale of that property at any time, even if the other one resists. It also permits the cash value of the property to be used to satisfy debt obligation incurred by either of the spouses.

Couples who want to leave their ownership share in the house to children from a former marriage should consider *tenants in common*. Then, in your will you declare who you want to leave your share of the house to. There are complications, though. What if the surviving spouse wants to remain in the house and the children want to sell it to redeem their inheritance? What if both the surviving spouse and the deceased's heirs want to sell it, but can't agree on a price? Dividing a bank account after a death is a lot simpler than dividing a house.

Spouses can own homes separately, as *individuals*. Sole owners can sell the house, mortgage it or will it without the consent of a spouse; they're in full control of the property. What they often find during times of divorce, however, is that unless the separate ownership was clearly spelled out in a prenuptial agreement, property they thought was separate is marital. When one of the partners owns the home and has grown children who he or she eventually wants to inherit the house, it makes sense to establish a marital life estate trust. It's a way of ensuring the surviving spouse the use and comfort of the home for as long as he or she lives. The surviving children are entitled to the property only after his or her death. (For more estate planning information, see chapter ten.)

MOVING IN

Marty and Darlene's desire for a place of their own was put on hold for a number of reasons. He had just taken a new job and didn't feel secure enough in it to risk a move that was certain to incur additional expenses.

Apart from finances, the most frequently cited reason for staying in a home that one of the spouses is not wanting to uproot children.

"They've had to deal with so much already," Esther says of her three school-age children, who found themselves fatherless two years ago when her husband was killed in a car accident. "They're dealing fairly well with the prospect of my remarriage. I don't want to move them and ask them to adjust to yet another trauma. Not now."

NEUTRALIZING THE GROUND

No matter how hard you try to block them out, ghosts of the past haunt the old residence.

A man moving into his new wife's home is told which closet is his—not because it's the one he wants, but because it's the one the man of the house has always had.

A woman wants to move some of the objects her husband collected with a former wife. He objects.

A man discovers the mortgage payments on his wife's condo are being paid for, in part, by his wife's former husband, who is half owner of the place. He feels like a "kept" man.

A stepparent is turned into an intruder by the kids who have been living in the house. "Who does he think he is, putting his desk into the den?" one angry stepson asked. "This is our house."

Countering the uncomfortable feelings of the newcomer and the proprietary feelings in-residence family members have when newcomers move in challenges the newly remarried couple's tact, sensitivity and creativity.

The stories that follow are from families who have done it and, in the process, have discovered some ways to make the process of blending easier.

"Sid didn't like the idea of sleeping in the same room my former husband and I slept in—nor did I, frankly. But what really jolted us into action was the fact that my daughter, Ellen, kept referring to our bedroom as 'yours and daddy's room.' We renovated the attic of the house and made it into a little apartment for ourselves. Ellen was given the choice of staying in her old room or claiming the master bedroom. She chose the master bedroom, and then painted and redecorated it. Her old room became the guest room her stepbrothers use when they visit. They were given the option to decorate that room any way they liked—within reason—and they plastered the walls with posters of their favorite rock stars."

STRATEGIES FOR NEUTRALIZING

Shuffle bedrooms. Bedrooms are the private areas in a home. Changing whose is whose makes you and the resident children feel like you're in a new place. It also helps to evict the ghosts.

Redecorate. Encourage children to redecorate, too. Don't expect that children will bring the same taste to a bedroom that you do, but give them as much latitude as you can afford (and stomach) to make their bedrooms uniquely theirs.

Assume a financial obligation for or buy into the house if you're the newcomer. Many divorce agreements state that one party, usually the wife, has the right to remain in the house until the kids are grown or until some other agreed-upon time, like the wife's remarriage. The property is then to be sold and the profits divided. A new husband, if he can afford it, can buy the former husband's half (either directly, or indirectly through his new wife). Even if he can't afford it outright, he and his wife can take out a home equity loan to pay off the former husband.

In Marsha's separation agreement with her former husband, she had the right to live in the house until her son reached the age of eighteen or she remarried—whichever came first. At that time, the house had to be sold to a third party or she had to buy her first husband out. Marsha and her fiancé Ray wanted to stay in the house. It would be better for her daughter, Marsha reasoned. Ray liked the idea because the house was close to his former wife's home where his children live for four of the seven days of the week. The other three days they are with him as part of his joint custody arrangement. The same bus would be able to drop the children off at either of their parent's homes.

Ray gave Marsha the $80,000 she needed to buy the other half of the house. A portion of it came from his savings. He borrowed the rest.

If one of the spouses owns the house outright, the other should take an active financial part in the upkeep of the residence. Perhaps it means writing out the mortgage check form one's own account or paying for the maintenance on the property. He or she *feels* a sense of ownership when the contribution is made. And indeed, the ownership would probably be viewed as real, if the couple were to separate and the matter went to court—even if the original owner's name remained on the deed.

Be alert to signs of any uneasiness your spouse might feel about this arrangement. It isn't easy to be the outsider in someone else's home. Don't use the powerful situation to lessen the influence, responsibility or decision-making capacity of your spouse.

"Without realizing it, I was always referring to the house as 'my house,'" Maddy confesses. "I'd tell people 'I' was putting an addition on 'my house'. Even though Paul was paying for it, I still felt in control. Paul felt it too, because at a business dinner I said 'my house' once too often and he exploded. We had a terrible fight. I wasn't sensitive to the discomfort Paul felt about living here, nor to his dislike over my possessiveness about the house I had living in for thirteen years."

Compromise so that each of you has enough of yourself in this house to make you both feel at home.

"I bought my dream house just months before the divorce from my second husband," Lynn says. For the next three years, while I was single again, I fixed it up just the way I wanted. Then I met Marvin. After his divorce he bought a broken-down home with a lot of history behind it. Over the years he renovated it and eventually got it on the historic register. He wanted me to move into his house; I wanted him to move into mind." It was, Lynn admits, the single most difficult issue they had to resolve when they married.

The compromise: Marvin moved in to Lynn's house, but he brought along his furniture.

MERGING TWO HOUSEHOLDS

I wonder if the eclectic look in household furnishing didn't jump into vogue when the divorce and remarriage rates skyrocketed! Merging two disparate styles can make for a fascinating look: a Hoosier cabinet housing a DVD player; a sleek leather sofa softened with needlepoint pillows; Currier and Ives prints grouped under halogen lighting.

Culling through the effects of two households to put together one exciting decor sounds intriguing, but even the most creative spirit finds it a nightmare sometimes. You have to work through your emotional connection to an object; your spouse must do the same. If there are children involved, you must move slowly when assessing items they consider theirs—like how many VCR's, beds or phone you need as you merge households. To a child undergoing upheaval as a result of the remarriage, even the kitchen table becomes "mine" and an object to fight over. Children, especially, want to hang on to the familiar, the comfortable and, most importantly, the life *before* the stepparent. Respect that (even if it galls you). Prior to disposing of excess equipment, furniture or appliances, give children who are old enough to make decisions a chance to sort through their own things, selecting what's meaningful to them and what they think they can part with.

"It was harder to dispose of my period furniture than I thought it would be," Charlotte reports. "When I tried to entice my adult children into taking different pieces, each and every one told me that they didn't like French provincial. I was a bit taken aback—considering they had lived with this style while they were growing up."

Discard as much as possible before you make the actual move so that you don't have to pay movers to tote items you're going to get rid of in a few months. Then dispose of the unwanted items using any of the following methods:

- Have a "cash and marry" garage sale and make some money from the duplicate items.
- Give the extras to relatives or to a charity.
- Auction or sell to dealers pieces of worth.
- Put furniture in storage, saving it for children when they're old enough to move into quarters of their own or for a second home that you plan to buy one day.

Carla, an Atlanta human resource administrator, had another reason for renting storage space. "When Joel and I got married eleven years ago, we were in love but not in trust. That's why I put all the duplicate items I brought into the household—furniture, washing machine, mixer, even a toaster—into storage rather than selling or giving them away. I had been badly hurt in my first marriage—both emotionally and financially—and I wasn't giving up 'my' things easily. My fear was 'What if we get a divorce?' As I grew more confident about the relationship, I started to sell off things. About five years into the marriage, I was out of storage."

Carla concludes: "When we replaced our dressers with built-in cabinets, I knew our marriage was solid."

Chapter Five

ABCs of Money Management:
Accounts, Budgets and Chores

"In my first marriage, I controlled the money and she controlled the sex. Neither of us was happy," says Arnie, a Savannah, Georgia, CPA. "Now Jan manages some money, I manage some, and neither of us really knows how much we have left at the end of the month. But that's fine with me," Arnie declares. "As for sex," he adds with a grin, "we both manage that."

Sex aside for the moment, we do handle our finances differently in a remarriage than we did in the first go-around. There's more sharing when it comes to decision-making. Women want more involvement this time, and men appear more eager to give up some of the responsibility, according to a study conducted by Marilyn Coleman, Professor and Chair of the Department of Human Development and Family Studies, and Lawrence Ganong, Associate Professor in the School of Nursing, both at the University of Missouri.

Shared decision-making bodes well for a remarriage. The sharing that happens as a result of positive communication should lessen the intensity and the frequency of money fights. I say "should" because sharing doesn't ensure tranquility. Increased financial responsibility and its inherent stress present a challenge to the balance of goodwill created by sharing.

"A" FOR ACCOUNTS

From the first electric bill and right on through tuition invoices, who pays for what is an issue in remarriage.

Most remarrieds start with a set of pots. An unmatched set.

One pot is his. One pot is hers. One might be theirs. One might be hers with a child. Or his with a child.

They might have his and her business pots. Pots with parents. Trust pots. Even pots with former spouses.

For the sake of reducing the pot tally, let's limit discussion to what I call the "One, Two, Three Pot Remarriage" system.

- The one-pot has all accounts (checking, savings and investments) in joint names.
- The two-pot has all accounts divided (rarely evenly) into his accounts and her accounts.
- The three-pot has a his account, a her account and a their account.

There's no right or wrong number of pots for a remarriage. You have to achieve a comfortable balance between your individual needs for independence and autonomy and commitment to the "common good" of the remarriage.

For Enid, a psychotherapist in Houston, and Dan, a manager in the international division of a Fortune 500 company, the two-pot set is a must.

"It's definitely a what's-mine-is-mine, what's-your-is-yours marriage," says Enid. "Not that we aren't both very generous to each other. We are. But I get pride out of handling my own finances and he feels the same way about his. If we had done the 'we' number, I would have become too vigilant about the way he spends money. I would be resentful when we spend large sums to bring his children up from Argentina twice a year.

"We've limited our financial expectation of each other. And therefore, we've limited our resentment," she says.

Women, especially those who experience a precipitous drop in income after a divorce, are often skittish about pooling funds.

"I was so badly stung, financially, when Albert and I split," says Faith, "that I can't bear the idea of a joint account that Bernie, my new husband, might be able to raid. If I were perfectly honest, I suppose I'd have to call this my 'get up and go' account in case this marriage fails."

Sharon represents the other end of the comfort scale. An advertising account executive on parental leave caring for their two small boys, she has been living with Peter, an art director, in London, New York, and now Los Angeles for the past thirteen years, and has been married to him for nine.

"We pooled our resources from the very beginning—even though Peter was in major hock, paying back all the debts from his past marriage," Sharon says. "My income was all we had."

Most remarried shift financial accounts from time to time simply because there's a difference in how you view your pot collection after five years of marriage, after ten, and after twenty. There's also a difference in how you view your pots if you have a child together, when a weekend-visiting-child becomes your permanent resident, and when all the children are grown.

The One-Pot System

Pooling all the income in a joint account from which expenses and investments are drawn seems to work best for young families with limited resources, for childless remarrieds, and for couples who have secure and long remarriages—so much so they can't even remember their "former lives." Very little negotiating has to be done with this arrangement. In remarried families where there are children, it has the psychological effect of saying that the money of the family is being committed to the common good of the family without regard to who comes from which family. And with regard to the spouses, it indicates there is no one adult who wields the power over finances.

"Let's face it. Neither of us has enough money to make a difference," says Dan, a thirty-five-year old Boston social worker, married for a year to Carol, a twenty-eight-year old social worker and mother of seven-year old Tony. "Anyway, I want Carol to feel that what's mine is hers. I want her to handle all the finances. It's not that I don't trust myself. I do. But I need her to trust me, and I'm still not sure that she does. She knows that I'm an addict with five years sobriety. If we have money in one account, Carol will always know what's there. If I had money in a separate account, she might wonder what I'm doing with 'my' money. I screwed up my first marriage and I have no intention of doing that again. Carol is special, and I feel like a father to Tony."

The Two-Pot System
Each of you keeps your income and accounts separate and each retains control over your individual expenditures. It's pretty tough to figure out who used what electricity or to pluck numbers from the phone bill to assess whose long distance calls were whose, so couples make accommodations. "The mortgage is your responsibility; utilities, mine." "Your children's room redecoration is yours; I'll pay for entertainment when my kids come visiting." Or they set up elaborate (and sometimes hysterically cumbersome) formulas. "Your two children live with us, but they only eat as

much as one adult, so you should pay two-thirds of the food costs and I'll pay one-third. And because we have to cart them places frequently, I'll assume one-fourth of the car costs; you handle the other three-fourths.

Couples with this setup are usually more affluent, may be older when they remarry, or have strong needs for personal autonomy. As a practical matter, if one of the spouses is heavily in debt when he or she remarries and fears not being able to pay off the indebtedness, then maintaining separate accounts helps to insulate the mate from having assets attached.

Problems and resentments build when there is an inequality in income and one partner winds up with a zero balance at the end of the month while the other still has plenty to spend. If this happens, it's time to consider moving to three pots.

Spouses in two-pot families have less positive feelings for the partner's children, the Coleman/Ganong study reports. Perhaps that's why the two accounts were established in the first place. Johnny's mom doesn't want her new husband looking over her shoulder questioning her generosity to her child. The problem is that by setting up the separate account, Johnny's mom frequently exacerbates her husband's resentment.

Does the two-pot system perpetuate divided loyalties? Probably. But it also offers autonomy and control to each spouse.

The Three-Pot System

The yours, mine and ours system of managing income and expenses is designed to bolster commitment by emphasizing the needs of the family as a whole, while also allowing each of you the freedom of a private fund. Each family puts its own spin on this system when it decides which items will be paid for individually and which jointly—and how much from each spouse's paycheck will go into each fund.

You can go about this one of two ways:

1. Pool all income in a joint account to pay for joint expenses, such as rent or mortgage, household expenses, entertainment, car expenses and purchases, doctor bills, and savings for emergency accounts. Then withdraw a set dollar amount that will go into each of your own personal accounts. Those accounts might then be responsible for child support payments, gifts for each spouse's family, miscellaneous personal expenses.

2. Put your paychecks into your own accounts and from them allocate a portion into a joint account to pay for rent or mortgage, the family car, entertainment, household expenses, doctor bills, and the like. You need to agree on what percentage of each paycheck will be put into the joint account.

Although some remarrieds will, over a period of years, move on to a single-pot system, most remain with some adaptation of the three-pot system. It seems to encompass the best of all worlds for people who are used to handling their own funds, but whose conversation is sprinkled with "we."

"In the early stages of our marriage, we were dogmatic about keeping our finances separate," Carla says of her fourteen-year marriage to Dennis, who had been married before. "We kept telling each other that we were totally committed to the marriage because we equated commitment to fidelity. But without realizing it, we held back. Not sexually. Monetarily. It wasn't until we opened a joint account, about six years after we were married, that we fully understood what the word 'commitment' meant."

B FOR BUDGET OVERVIEW

Ban the "B" word if when you hear it you think of deprivation, restriction, limits, quotas, or martyrdom. But when you want to buy a new car and need to find the money for it or take the whole family on vacation and have to determine whether you have to sell stock to finance it, you'll need to get a handle on what's coming in and what's going out—an overview of your finances. This *Budget Overview* is really a spending plan. (Cash analysis, another term for the same thing, sounds like you're in a business together—but that's probably not how you operate.)

In a Budget Overview you look at the situation as if you were peering down at a chessboard. You can assess where the pieces are, and you can move them to fit your own family's needs. You plan for the long term, but since you never know the next move life is going to make, you remain flexible.

Most appealing about a Budget Overview is that when you're all finished you don't try to squeeze yourself into someone else's assessment of how things ought to be. Remarried couples and stepfamilies aren't like others. There are financial pulls and pushes that nuclear families don't experience. So you have to create oddball financial plans that may be molded around quickie weekends at romantic inns to coincide with a child's visit to a noncustodial parent, reupholstering the furniture from a "former life" to match new tastes, and astronomical long distance phone charges to stay close to children who don't live with you.

Putting the Pieces Together
How much are you earning and how much are you spending? Most people know approximately what they earn (thanks to the assessment forced by the IRS each April). But few could come within a few thousand dollars

of what they really spend, if they were simply to guess. This is especially true in a remarriage because the new union is not accustomed to the expenses that aren't listed in traditional budgets, such as children's travel expenses when they visit noncustodial parents, entertainment when they visit you, expenses agreed to under a separation agreement, additional gifts as a result of having a swollen family tree or guilt over divorcing a child's mother.

> *An auctioneer from St. Louis was dumbfounded when he went back over his checkbook to calculate just how much he had spent during the past year on his two teenage children who were living with their mother in the same city. "Under my separation agreement," he relates, "I must pay $25,000 in support. In reality, when you count the hockey uniforms, braces for my daughter's teeth, and Christmas, birthday and what I call 'guilt-driver' presents, I spent $41,000 on my children."*

Do you know how much you spend each year? Without going back to the checkbook or canceled checks, or without going to the computer program which tallies everything up, take a guess.

To find out just how close you are to the actual figure, do one of two things. The first is to get a computer program such as Quicken, which, as long as you remember to enter all the transactions, will keep track of your expenditures and deposits. The second is to do the same thing the computer would do—only manually.

Keep track of everything you spend and earn over a three-month period. Place every expenditure into a category. At a minimum you'll want these categories:

- Basic Housing Costs (rent/mortgage; taxes; insurance; utilities; water; fuel, etc.)
- Telephone

- Housing Upkeep (repairs; furniture; equipment; appliances; household help)
- Groceries
- Meals Out
- Entertainment for the two of you
- Clothing (purchases; cleaning)
- Transportation (everything you spend on a car; subway and bus fares)
- Travel (vacations; airfare; hotels; car rentals)
- Education (for you and your kids)
- Medical (the difference between what is covered and what you spend for doctors, hospitals, drugs, etc; insurance premiums)
- Family (childcare; child support; allowances; recreation)
- Savings and investments (all pension and retirement plan contributions; all investments, including real estate
- Charity and gifts
- Debt (interest and principal payments you're making monthly)
- Taxes (federal, state and local)
- Personal (pocket money that's hard to keep track of)

To make life simple for yourself, keep as little cash in your pocket as possible and pay for almost everything by check or credit card. That includes meals out, commutation tickets, childcare expenses, cleaning, even groceries. That way, when you get your monthly bank statement and credit card bills, you'll have a record of what you've spent and you can record anything you forgot to record.

Don't forget to add up what's on the other side of the proverbial ledger: income. Include what ever is applicable: salaries, proceeds from the sale of assets, rental income, income from trusts or estates, Social Security or pension income, child support.

At the end of the three months, tally up your expenses that have been categorized and your income. If you multiply those totals by four, you should get a general idea of your annual income and annual expenses.

Remember: Expenditures Change

Yes, it's possible (even probable) that your former spouse will remarry and you'll be spared alimony payments, or that your son will come live with you and your new spouse and your former spouse will refuse to contribute to his support. You might have children of your own. The shifting households of remarried families and the passage of time make change inevitable. But having an overview of what's going on in your financial life allows you to move the pieces of puzzle around with more confidence. If you know you'll be saving $10,000 a year on alimony, you'll be able to allocate the money to another category. If you're aware that having another child in the household will mean an additional $8,000 the first year, you'll be able to see where to move money from to cover that expense.

The B Word Resurfaces

If you can remember that budgets are made to fit people and not the other way around, you won't gag on the B word. But saying it doesn't mean you have to put it down on paper. Once you've done the Budget Overview, most people can figure out how they're doing—expenses vs. income—without keeping a running written record. I know I risk scorn from financial planners of the type-A variety, but unless there is some dramatic change in circumstances or your expenses-to-income ratio is out of whack, you don't have to do the overview more than once every couple of years. Formal, annual reports to yourself are good only if they make you feel more comfortable. If they loom like monsters, skip a year. And once you've been married for a few years, you'll be able to predict with some accuracy the changes that will be occurring (such as the end of formal support) and adjust to them.

If there doesn't seem to be a way you can live year to year without gnawing at savings or going into debt, you'll find strategies for reversing the flow in the chapter "When There's Not Enough."

C FOR CHORES

Financial decision-making should be shared.

But who pays the bills, fills out forms for a mutual fund account, gets papers ready for the accountant and fights with a credit card company over a bill—that's another matter.

Forget gender. Who likes to do those tasks? If you both do, split them up or take turns—switching every six months. If one of you has an accountant's love of detail and wouldn't miss a reconciliation session with a bank statement for all the chips in tollhouse cookies, bless him or her.

But if the chores have fallen, by default, to one of you who has little time or love for them, be creative in your approach to the task. Options include:

1. Calculating how many hours a week it takes to keep the family finances under control, and trading off some of your other responsibilities (such as mowing the lawn, picking the kids up from Sunday school, or grocery shopping) with your spouse.
2. Paying yourself for the chore with time alone—and letting your spouse know that that's what you're doing so he or she can take over parenting or housekeeping chores during that time.
3. Devising the simplest financial recordkeeping system you can, because if you feel overwhelmed or if your expensive, sophisticated computer system has a learning curve that's too long, you'll lose interest and do nothing.

4. Practicing one of the following chore-dodging ploys that either shorten the length of time you'll spend on task or eliminate it altogether. (And don't let anyone make you feel guilty about these. Bankers, lawyers and CPA use them.) Ploys include:

- *Not balancing your checkbook.* Or at least not doing it every month. Heresy, you say? Why? Is it really important to know to the penny how much you have? If you can't keep a fairly accurate running total in your head, call the bank, punch into the automatic teller machine once in a while, or do online banking. Two precautionary measures in case your mental math fails: Pad your account with a $100 unrecorded deposit, and set up an overdraft account—really a line of credit. The one checking chore you must do: Record all deposits.

- *Rounding checks and balances up to the nearest dollar.* Who needs to spend time adding up pennies (unless you're using a computer program that makes it all seem easy)? This ploy also gives you a small financial cushion that protects against error.

- *Closing your account and starting over.* This is akin to having your house repainted when the task of washing the walls seems overwhelming. It seems a little extreme, but I know people who swear by it.

- *Hiring someone to take care of your finances.* You don't have to be mentally incompetent to cry for help. One couple said that hiring a financial manager literally saved their marriage because they no longer fought over who did what…and they had more quality time together.

Chapter Six

When There's Not Enough

Even today, when both husband and wife usually work, remarried households with children living at home are the worst off, economically, relative to other married family types.

Financial strains common in remarriages aren't calibrated just on how much the couple earns. Financial *pressure* is also part of the measurement. When you live up to what you earn (and many people do), you feel all the money earned is needed. Suppose, for example, an annual household income is $95,000 and $25,000 of that has always been sent to a custodial parent for child support. When that support obligation ceases, the unshackled $25,000 is used to buy a much-needed car or to fund a retirement plan. It's rarely spent on a new wardrobe or dinners out for the next five years. With the exception of the very wealthy, people always have a "need" for money, though needs change. And it's ridiculous to get into a contest over who has the greatest need—even though you always have to make decisions about allocating resources. Is a stepchild's private school need greater than your need for a vacation? Or is your need for a new suit less meaningful than your spouse's need to join a health club? These are personal decisions, of course, to be made on a case-by-case basis.

Pair ongoing money squeezes with the financial emergencies that may strike any family from time to time, and problems compound. One of you is downsized or unable to work for an extended time; the family is hit with an enormous, unexpected expense. How do you handle the times of financial trouble?

The defensive and offensive strategies that follow will help. But as a government official said of the year he was out of work as a result of a layoff, grit and a supportive spouse are the secrets to getting through the tough times. "If Molly had been the same type as my former wife, I probably would have hung myself by now. But her optimistic attitude, quiet pullback in spending, and constant encouragement helped me pull through."

THE ONGOING SQUEEZE

Dick, a San Diego-based marketing manager, visualizes the pressures of supporting two families this way: "It's as if a hose were attached to my checking account, steadily drawing out money." He's at the point that whenever he writes a check that's not part of his fixed expenses, he tenses up, certain he'll go into debt. To his first family, he's legally bound; to his second, he's financially strapped.

Children are squeezes extraordinaire. They are more expensive than statistics indicate, especially in upper-income families where parents are eager to give children more—more education, more lessons, more clothes, more material goods. And children, whether hers, his, or theirs, give the word "unforeseen" an expensive cast. Unforeseen natural ability as an up-and-coming Tiger Woods, for example, puts pressure on parents and stepparents to buy equipment, pay for lessons, and ante up for transportation to and from amateur tournaments. Children continue to have unforeseen injuries, doctors' bills or special needs all throughout their growing-up years.

State laws generally relieve stepparents of financial responsibility for their stepchildren, except when the children are, or are about to become, public charges. The primary financial responsibility is on the biological parents. But real life isn't that neat. You marry someone. Your lives entwine. Even if you try to insulate yourself, you find yourself feeling responsible for your stepchildren. As time goes on, you might grow to love them. And then the question is not who's responsible for what, but what can you afford and what do you want to do for the children.

When there's not enough money, resentment can erupt. Often one partner feels too much of the joint funds are being used to meet the financial needs of a prior marriage. Worse still is when a new spouse feels his or her personal funds are being drained by the obligations of the other spouse.

Stepfathers, especially, get tapped. They are frequently asked to contribute to stepchildren's financial well being when a wife's former husband skips out on paying. (The errant parent rationalizes it this way: "My former wife has remarried. Now let someone else foot the bills." Unfortunately, too many fathers feel this way—perhaps they're jealous of a new man usurping their role in the lives of their children.)

Stepmothers who are financially independent and who bring no children of their own to the new marriage frequently find themselves contributing to the support of a former wife who refuses to work or can't. Says an ad agency executive who buys clothes for her two stepchildren every time they visit:

"I hate that woman [the children's mother]. She sends them to us looking like ragamuffins and tells them to ask us for clothes because she doesn't have enough money to buy them herself. Considering what my husband doles out for support, her actions are appalling. I end up paying for everything in our marriage because most of what he makes goes to the kids. As a result, we're still renting, though we should have bought a condo a long time ago."

The squeeze continues, and resentment boils when a husband or wife feels the former spouse isn't participating in the support of the children.

"My ex has made an art of avoiding full-time employment," Dennis complains bitterly. "If she earned anything, she'd take some of the pressure off me." Says Dennis's second wife, a magazine editor with no children of hr own, "On

a good day in a good year, I don't mind chipping in or having Dennis con-tribute most of his earnings to care for his children and first wife. We have always had enough. But this year was a shaky financial one for both of us. I'm annoyed that Dennis doesn't say something to force her into taking a job and contributing to the kids' support."

When can you tell that the strain is too great?

WARNING SIGNS

Recognizing early signs of trouble and responding to them swiftly is the best defense against months that stretch further than a paycheck. The financial squeeze is on when you:

- Feel as if you're losing control of your life
- Use savings to pay current expenses
- Postdate checks to keep them from bouncing
- Send less support/alimony than you are obligated to, are constantly late with it, or fail to send it altogether
- Continually dip into the credit line of your checking account
- Regularly exceed the borrowing limit on your credit cards
- Use cash advances from some credit cards to pay off others
- Pay only the minimum monthly balance due on credit cards
- Borrow money from friends and relatives for current expenses

What can you do to ease the financial pressure?

Remarried couples have the same fiscal choice as others caught in a financial vise: Spend less or earn more. They also have the recourse of going after a parent who's not providing the agreed-upon support. Support-payers can cut the outflow by reducing support.

SPEND LESS

Clearly the first step for couples who chronically overspend is to do an overview of their budget with an eye toward shaving expenses in nonessential areas. Spending cuts should be a joint task. No one person should be the martyr, sacrificing his or her comforts or resources for the good of everyone else.

Each partner must review his or her own expenditures, making reductions that reflect individual priorities. Dick said he was willing to brown-bag lunch a few times a week but didn't want to forgo his health club membership, which was reasonably priced by neighborhood standards. His wife felt her fashionable haircut couldn't be done by anyone but her expensive stylist, but she could do her own nails occasionally and cut down on the manicurist bills.

Decisions on joint expenses are up for discussion and negotiation. Examine each section of your budget for a possible reduction of living expenses. If the imbalance of income to expenses is only slight, simple fine-tuning is all you need: postponing the purchase of a new car for six months, eating one less meal out every week, or giving less elaborate gifts to each other or family members. Facing a problem together and finding creative solutions can defuse the feelings of despair or helplessness and give more padding to the middle ground needed for a successful remarriage.

Instead of being ushered to a posh restaurant table once a week, Dick and Donna, for example, have found more ingenious and less costly ways to be alone. They pack a wacky combination of childhood favorite foods and drive to the coast where they watch the sun set as they down "fluffernutter" sandwiches and milk. When possible, they exchange babysitting time with another couple and when they're "off," they spend the evening at home alone.

TEN EASY, EFFICIENT "GET SMART" IDEAS

Investigate these suggestions immediately. They're valuable even if you don't need to prune expenses.

Insurance

1. *Chip away at your car insurance premium.* Quiz your agent about ways to lower the premium: high deductible, installation of alarm systems and air bags, discounts for good driving, and elimination of collision coverage on an old car.

2. *Take advantage of your universal life policy.* If you've been paying premiums regularly, this might be the time to cash in on the flexibility of the policy by using your cash reserve. Check your yearly statement or call you broker to find out if you have enough in reserve to do this without affecting the amount of your coverage.

Credit

3. *Empty your wallet or purse of credit cards.* Pay off the outstanding balances on all but two of the cards. Put those two cards back into your wallet for emergency use. With your final payment to the other credit card companies, send a note saying you no longer want the card and return it cut up. Savings accrue immediately. No more yearly fees on those cards.

4. *Search for a bankcard with an interest rate lower than what you're now paying.* You might have to pay an annual fee of $25 or $50, but even that will be considerably lower than the monthly interest charges on $1,000.

Taxes and Financial Services

5. *Do your own tax returns.* With last year's return in hand, do this year's—aided by one of the annual step-by-step tax guides by J.K. Lasser, H&R Block, or the Dummy's Series, available in bookstores at the end of January. Even the IRS's free booklet "Your Federal Income Tax" will help. (Find it on the Web at *www.irs.gov* or get it by calling 800-829-1040.)

Don't forget: The parent with physical custody for the greater portion of the year has the right to list children as dependents, even though he or she may not provide the majority of the support. For the IRS to recognize a different arrangement, the custodial parent must sign a form waiving his or her right to the exemption. The form then must be attached to the other parent's tax return.

6. *Don't pay for what you can get for free.* Many financial services are free: no-fee checking accounts, no-load mutual funds, and no-annual-fee credit cards. And even if your financial services institution doesn't advertise free services, approach them asking if they have them. In many cases, they can make special arrangements, especially if you've been a long-standing customer.

7. *Use money market accounts and funds to pay bills of more than $250.* If you're keeping the money you need for monthly expenditures in a no-interest checking account, transfer some money to a money market account at your bank (most allow you to write at least three large checks a month without charge) or a money market fund at a mutual fund or brokerage firm (most have a dollar minimum of $250 per check, but no minimum on the number of checks you write). That way you'll be earning interest while the money is waiting to be paid out.

Spending

8. *Quit carrying your ATM card.* If it's not in your wallet, you're not tempted to drop into the bank to withdraw money. That helps reduce impulse buying. Take as much from your paycheck as you think you'll need until the next pay period. Spend only what you have in your wallet.

9. *Eliminate all but the absolutely necessary major expenses this year.* Pamper your old car and learn to live with your VCR and dream about the DVD.

10. *Stop saving.* Sounds like strange advice, but this is not the time to worry about contributing to a company retirement plan so that you can save on taxes. Taxes are not your problem. Your first goal is to bring your day-to-day expenses into line.

EARN MORE

Even in tough financial times, careers flourish. Be aware of possible areas of promotion within your own company, and stay in touch with associates throughout the industry, with an eye to spotting an opportunity for advancement that would carry with it a hike in salary.

What about the added income from a second job? That might sound like a sensible idea when a couple is strapped for money, but for couples in the early stages of a remarriage, it can be threatening. Time as a couple and time as a family are as precious as money for a new marriage. Weigh your answers to the following questions before taking on another job:

- Will being away from each other (or the family) be more of a strain than cutting back on expenditures? Consider that others in the family might have to pick up additional responsibilities as a result of one of the adults being away more. Too, there is less time together, which means less time to develop a common middle ground, and less time to meet the emotional needs of the members of this new family.
- Can the drain on your time and energy be limited? Can you moonlight just long enough to tide you over a rough spot, or must you do this for as long as you can foresee?
- How will the extra income affect your taxes?
- What are the additional costs (transportation, clothes, meals out, payment for home services such as housework, gardening, maintenance, additional childcare) associated with earning this extra income?
- Can you start a small business from your home that allows you to work together? For couples in the early stages of a remarriage who need to nurture the relationship, turning a hobby or service into additional income can be fun and profitable "togetherness." Children can be brought in to help, giving them a sense of belonging to this new family unit. But keep in mind that not all families are meant to work together; for some, it's a disaster.

Also remember that starting a venture is risky business. So be certain the business you're contemplating will be as risk-free as possible—perhaps a service you can provide that doesn't require a large capital outlay. Self-employed people have many tax breaks—not the least of which is being able to deduct expenses for that portion of your home used exclusively for business.

REDUCE SUPPORT FOR CHILDREN FROM A FORMER MARRIAGE

Reducing support sounds heartless, and sometimes it is. But not always. Suppose the company you work for closes its doors—no warning, no severance, no benefits. It happens. Even though your former spouse would probably challenge it, you could argue that if you were not divorced and remarried, your first family would still have to cut back its spending and retrench because of the situation.

If you petition the court to modify support payments for your noncustodial children, you might win. You usually must prove there's been a substantial change in your financial position—one that was not anticipated when the original payments were set. States vary in how they view remarriage when considering a reduction in support payments. Most deny modification simply because a noncustodial parent remarries, holding that earlier obligations come first.

Though it may be absolutely necessary, the decision to seek reduction of support should never by made lightly. Emotional ramifications resound—even when the reduction is reasonable and appropriate under the circumstances. More often than not, children see it as further abandonment, and former spouses use it to reemphasize the unworthiness of the noncustodial parent. And it's costly. You wind up spending thousands on legal fees—money that could otherwise be used for support or for righting your own financial position.

Just because a child switches households and comes to live you and your new spouse, don't assume the court will permit a reduction in child support to your former wife. A father of three tells this story.

"When my oldest child, Margie, came to live with us, I thought it was perfectly reasonable to ask my former wife to voluntarily agree to a reduction in child support. She didn't. Was I angry. I got a lawyer and appealed to the

court. But because my income had risen since the separation agreement was signed six years before, the court didn't think a reduction was appropriate. I lost the appeal. And probably should have. I used the support issue to infuriate my former wife because, quite honestly, I can't stand her."

Other states—other judges—might have made different determinations. Some do consider the expenses of second families, the contribution of the new spouse to those expenses, the support given to stepchildren, or any increased ability of the custodial parent to assume more of the financial responsibility.

FLUSH OUT THE ERRANT PARENT

Child support isn't an issue that can be argued. Parents who sign separation agreements pledging a certain level of support (and even those who don't) are responsible for financial support—unless there is some good reason why they can't provide it.

If a noncustodial parent neglects or disregards his or her parental responsibility, you have two courses of action. You can hire an attorney and bring the case to court, or you can apply for child support enforcement (CSE) services. The private attorney route is more expensive (and when the shortage of money is a problem, cost is an important consideration).

CSE legislation operates on federal and state levels. At the federal level, the Office of Child Support Enforcement (OCSE) administers it. At the state level, responsibility may be in any local agency, but frequently it's found in the social services or human resources departments. Once you've contacted the division that handles child support enforcement in your state, you have two routes—through the courts or through an administrative process.

The courts offer a wider range of enforcement remedies, such as civil contempt and possible jail terms for the errant parent. The administration process offers quicker service and is less costly because you don't have court costs or attorney fees. CSE can enforce payment by seizing wages, imposing liens, intercepting state tax refunds, making the delinquency known to any consumer credit bureau asking for the information, and allowing the federal government to garnish wages, pension benefits, and retirement pay (including Social Security). Be forewarned however. While child support receives some emphasis, the efforts of the state focus on helping children who are or who are about to become public charges.

All Fathers Are Not Contemptible

It's important to remember that all fathers who don't pay support on time or as much as they should aren't deadbeats.

Jarvis, an engineer in Houston, isn't a deadbeat. He was hauled into court by his former wife because he was $1,900 behind in support, even though he had told her that he and his wife had both lost their jobs (within three months of each other) and that he'd be reducing support for his six-year old son until he could find another position. Once he found a job, he would make up the deficit, he pledged. Although his former wife was remarried and living in her new husband's home, she proceeded with court action. The outcome: Jarvis had to pay his attorney $2,800 as well as paying an extra $200 a month to his former wife toward arrearages. "That wiped out a quarter of our savings," he said. His former wife paid her attorney $3,600. "Had she ridden out the hard times with he," he continued, "we both would have benefited—not the lawyers."

TIMES OF BIG TROUBLE

"One month before our marriage and after we closed on a house that we and four children (two of hers and two of mine) were going to be living in, my company laid off half of its employees. I was one of them," says Evan, a Georgia CPA. "We went ahead with our wedding plans because we figured Alice's position as assistant controller for a mid-sized company was secure. I also figured that I'd be employed shortly and that we'd be able to sell our two homes at a substantial profit quickly.

"It took me much longer to get a job than I anticipated. Ten months. And almost immediately the real estate market collapsed. Our respective homes are still on the market—20 months later. Even though Alice is still working, this has been a financial nightmare."

If You Have Some Warning

Sometimes you see the possibility of financial danger. For example, you're expecting a child and know that for a year or two you're going to be living on one income. Or perhaps one of you is in the process of making a career change that is sure to cause a blip in income.

Sometimes you sense danger. For example, you might see the company president and treasurer closeted in meetings and hear rumors that the company is on the verge of bankruptcy. Or your former spouse's regular support checks come later and later each month and are less than they should be.

If you see or sense trouble, take preventative measures immediately:

* *Do everything you would do if you were in a budget squeeze.* Ferret out the "must spends"—rent or mortgage utilities, food, and support/alimony. Then create a crisis budget and follow it.

- *Establish a line of credit.* Apply for a home equity loan that you can tap into if necessary. The good thing about this type of loan as opposed to others is that interest payments are tax-deductible.
- *Make certain a portion of your assets is liquid.* That way, if you have to sell something in a hurry you'll be able to. Don't put any new money into a certificate of deposit (CD) which will penalize you for an early withdrawal or into real estate, which is difficult to sell on short notice. And if you do have extra funds now, make certain they're in income-oriented, liquid investments.

When Crisis Blindsides You

Consider these scenarios. You walk into your office anticipating the day ahead and your supervisor tells you that he's sorry but the boss's nephew is replacing you. You must be out by 5 p.m.

Your spouse and stepchildren are in a terrible car accident. Your spouse will be out of work for at least six month and will need home care, which must be paid for out-of-pocket. Your medical coverage will only partially cover the medical expenses.

Here's how to minimize the financial damage:

- Do everything you would have done had you seen it coming.
- Call creditors and refinance or renegotiate loans. While it's tempting to hope creditors won't notice that you're in arrears, they do. Before you get a disconnect notice from the phone company, call and/or write to explain the problem. Most companies will accommodate you by accepting partial payment, converting you to a balanced billing system that spreads payments out equally over the year, or rescheduling the date you receive your bill. With a large debt, such as a car loan, some creditors will agree to stretch out your loan, thus reducing monthly payments. The rationale behind the creditor's apparent largess: A payment, even it's partial, is better than standing in bankruptcy bushes trying to retrieve what's owed.

One writer whose book advance didn't stretch as long as his auto loan payments was able to renegotiate his loan. Knowing he would be getting a substantial sum when the manuscript was accepted, he made a deal with the bank that required him to pay only interest until a single balloon payment of principal came due at the end of the loan period, which was a few months after he was to receive the lump-sum payment for the book.

- Call the institution holding your mortgage. Banks are not eager to foreclose on property that could be hard to unload. So let your bank know of your problem. Together you might be able to work out a temporary solution—perhaps reduced payments drawn out over a longer period.

  Having no choice but to close their scuba equipment store, a remarried couple was able to convince the savings and loan institution holding the mortgage on their house to suspend payments for a few months, giving them an opportunity to find jobs. (In fact, the Florida savings and loan even put them in touch with a distributor who eventually bought their inventory.) If you're renting, try to strike a deal with your landlord. In some cities eviction is a long process that landlords would rather not go through, especially when they're dealing with well-meaning tenants who are going through hard times.

- Involved the members of all families. First, try to renegotiate support/alimony obligations with a former spouse. If you have a civil relationship and your position is clear and just, she or he may be willing to agree to a temporary reduction of support or alimony rather than run the risk of having nothing and then having to start legal proceedings to retrieve the obligation. Said one San Francisco woman about her former husband's bankruptcy: "What can I do? He's distraught about the failure of his bookstore. He's a good father, even if he was a lousy husband. I know he'll start the child support again as soon as he gets on his feet. Until then, my husband and I will take over the full support of the kids. We're lucky. We're in a position to do that without much problem."

Second, if as the custodial parent you're the one in the bind, and you have reason to believe the support you're receiving from you child's other parent can be increased, ask him or her for it—on a temporary basis. Sometimes it's even possible to negotiate some future benefit, such as agreeing to give him more than one-half of the proceeds from a jointly owned house that you will sell at some later date.

Third, talk to the children—those living with you and those who depend on you for support. Children are likely to be confused and resentful during this stressful period. They may even think they're causing the problems. Without scaring them or making them feel responsible for coming up with solutions, discuss the situation.

An upstate New York high school administrator tells of the time, shortly after his remarriage, that he told his teenage children and stepchildren that he was resigning as principal of a school because he felt the situation was intolerable and detrimental to his health. He explained the politics and principles behind his reasoning and then outlined how he thought the decision would impact the family.

"I told them all that though I was a bit anxious about the decision, I was fully confident that our financial existence would be back on track in a year. Until then, though, I explained that we would have to cut back on spending. The family vacation we had planned for the summer would have to be postponed. Dinners out would be curtailed so would any clothing expenditures— except necessities.

"I was amazed at how they responded," he says. "They all seemed to want to help. Of the three, two immediately started looking for after-school jobs and once they had them, assured me I could discontinue their allowances and they'd

be just fine. All became more thoughtful about spending money—at least until I found another position."

This is not an unusual situation. Very frequently children see trouble as a rallying point and close ranks behind you so they can feel as if they're part of the new family. It all depends upon the ages of the children and how the adults handle the situation, however.

- List all the assets you can liquidate. Sell anything you don't value—from the diamond necklace stashed underneath the stock certificates in the safe-deposit box to the piano that hasn't been played or tuned for three years. Be certain to check with family members before selling these items, though. Especially in remarriages, spouses and children have important emotional attachments to material things. In a case where one of the parents has died and the other parent has remarried, for example, the piano may be the focal point of the child's memories of his deceased parent. In that case, the piano isn't an item you're likely to sell.

  Consider selling stocks, savings bonds, a third car, or a boat—anything you can replace when you're on firmer financial ground.
- Tap into hidden assets. Some assets that don't readily spring to mind may be tapped or borrowed against. For example, look into borrowing against the value of a corporate pension or profit-sharing plan within federal limits.

  If necessary, you can invade to Individual Retirement Account (IRA). The government does not limit the amount you can withdraw, although you'll pay income tax at current rates on any funds you remove before you reach fifty-nine-and-a-half, plus a 10 percent penalty. But there are exceptions. The penalty doesn't apply if you're withdrawing money to pay medical expenses in excess of 7 1/2 percent of your income. Additionally, anyone receiving unemployment for 12 consecutive weeks can withdraw money to pay health insurance premiums without paying the penalty. Self-employed people out of work for 12 weeks can also make penalty-free withdrawals to pay their health insurance premiums. Penalty-free withdrawals are also allowed for the purchase of a first home and to pay college expenses.

Banks won't lend you money if you're in dire financial straits, but if you can negotiate a loan before you're perceived as a poor credit risk, do it. Extend your overdraft checking privileges at the bank and increase the limits on your credit cards. (If you've been a reliable customer up to this point, banks and credit card issuers often do this without asking questions.)

• Investigate benefit options. If you or your spouse has been laid off or has a medical disability, ask the employer's benefits officer about the availability of payments from corporate, federal, state and local funds. Keep in mind that unemployment benefits are fully taxable.

If you lose your job and have vested pension benefits, you can take the money out of the plan now rather than rolling it over to an IRA or new pension plan. If you do, you'll pay current taxes on the distribution plus a 10 percent penalty tax for early withdrawal. (If you need the money, you need it!) No penalty tax is imposed if the money is withdrawn as a result of death, disability or severe medical problems, or if you're fifty-nine-and-a-half or older.

A CHANCE TO GROW

Being pummeled by the anxiety of tense times hurts. But those husbands and wives who supported each other and made it through the financial beatings say that, though they could have done without the problems, the relationship is stronger for the experience. Without exception, when the spouses reflected on the past woes, they wound up with renewed respect for one another.

Chris, forty-three, the only one of three siblings in the family business, had been assured by his father that he would receive sufficient equity in the business to ensure a smooth succession when the father retired. Chris relayed that assurance to Marie during their two-and-a-half year courtship—although he was somewhat concerned that no concrete plans were made to back up the promise. About the time he proposed to Marie, his father died. The bulk of the business and the entire building housing it were left to his mother. Chris had the mere 10 percent ownership stake he had been given when his father was alive.

Chris offered to buy his mother out. Even though he had increased sales ten times since his father's semi-retirement, and even though his mother had played no part in the business when her husband was alive, his mother was intransigent about relinquishing ownership and control.

Marie operates a small management consulting firm that she had painstakingly nurtured over the four and a half years since her divorce. She had been looking forward to being a wife and mother again—even having another child—and to devoting more time to her creative side—composing music. "Money symbolizes security to me," she explains, "though I never have chosen a man or followed a career path because of it.

"I would have liked to have had the issue of ownership settled before our wedding," Marie says, "but since that didn't seem likely, I reasoned that there was no optimum time to get married, so we'd wed as planned in July. After all, we loved each other.

"I sent the invitations out. About a week later, without discussing it with me, Chris resigned from the family business."

"I had taken two days off to get ready for the wedding," Chris explains. "The people in the office were quite competent to run it without my being there. When I got back there were four messages that my mother had called. I called her back and she started berating me for my absence. I told her that if she thought she could run the business better, perhaps this would be a good

time for her to try. I sent her what I thought was a reasoned letter of resigna-tion—which was accepted without comment—and I left the business two weeks later."

Chris opened a small export business with clients he had developed over the years. *"Exporting was a side business for my mother's company and there was no one there who knew the clients or anything about the subject but me,"* he says. *"I didn't raid her company for any domestic customers. I could have, but I didn't think it was the honorable thing to do."*

For about nine months, Chris's business did well. Chris's mother liquidated her company at about the same time Chris's orders started to slip—though there didn't seem to be any connection between the two events.

Struggling to keep his business alive long enough for a big deal to come through, Chris borrowed money from the bank using the house he owned with his former wife as collateral. She agreed to sign for a home equity loan with him as long as he paid it off. But business proceeded to get worse. And since he had to stop drawing income from it, he stopped paying alimony and support. He got sick and was hospitalized for a while. Then, not able to keep the busi-ness afloat any longer, Chris closed it and started looking for a job.

During that year and a half, Marie took on the financial responsibility for their life together. *"I was angry because I was draining my business of capital. I was angry because I never had had any threatening creditors calling my house before. I was angry because though I consider myself an enlightened woman, I hadn't expected this to be a one-sided deal,"* Marie admits.

"And I panicked. Although Chris was doing what he was supposed to do to find a job, I kept thinking, 'Let him drive a cab. Let him do something.'"

Marie didn't want anger and panic to destroy her marriage, especially since she was sympathetic to his position. She sought the help of a behavioral thera-pist, who pointed out that the reason Chris wasn't contributing to the family's finances might be because he didn't have to. *"I was keeping everything on an even keel,"* Marie says. *"The therapist asked me what I thought would be a fair contribution for me to make to the family. I said I thought it was fair to*

take care of the mortgage, food, and the upkeep of the house, but that any dis-
cretionary expenditures—the housekeeper, entertainment, new clothes—
should be Chris's responsibility."

"Marie and I talked about this," Chris continues. "I hated the idea of
applying for unemployment benefits, but I also hated asking her for money. I
realized that I needed to contribute to the family, even while I was waiting for
the job offer that I was sure would come. So I went through the humbling
experience of waiting in an unemployment insurance line.

"I felt better after that," Chris says. "And it took the pressure off Marie."

"There is no doubt that our relationship started healing from the trauma
we experienced during the last eighteen months when Chris started to con-
tribute to the household financially," Marie says.

Chris's optimism and persistence paid off. He now has a well-paying mana-
gerial position, which allows him to flex his entrepreneurial muscle. There's
almost a palpable sigh of relief from both of them when they talk about the
next few years. Chris's debt of more than $160,000 must be repaid, and that
will drain him of most of his income over the next three years. But then he'll be
able to lend meaningful financial support to this remarriage. Marie and Chris
acknowledge they still have problems. But they have come through a major
financial crisis and are still committed to each other. "I feel proud of us for
that," Marie says.

DEFUSING ANGER

When money pressures become too great, there are practical steps you can
take to defuse the resentment and safeguard your finances.

Air Your Feelings

Use the talk techniques in chapter two. Forget the legalities for a moment.
Talk about how much financial responsibility you feel you should have for

your marriage or your spouse's obligations from a former marriage, and why you feel infuriated by using your funds to pay off debts.

"When Aaron was out of work, I had a full-time managerial job and was writing a book," Sylvia said. "Resentment overwhelmed me. I told him I just couldn't keep pouring funds into his children's education. While I love those kids, I do feel they're his charges, not mine. I needed to have some money that I could assign to my own personal goals. Aaron agreed that we needed to find a fairer solution."

Don't Write Checks for Obligations That Aren't Yours

Even if you wind up paying for them in the long run, have your spouse write the check for his or her obligations from your joint account. Or give your check to your spouse for his or her personal account. Either way, you spouse will have the responsibility of paying the obligation personally. Aaron satisfied Sylvia's need to disassociate herself from providing money for his children by taking out a small home equity loan.

Aaron put the money in his account, and I never involved myself with his children's finances again," Sylvia said. "We reached a verbal agreement that he would repay the loan when he was working again. And he did. I can't tell you what a difference that made in how I felt."

Be Empathetic…and as Financially Supportive as Possible

Losing a business or losing a job is a blow to everyone, but it's most severe to the person it's happening to.

Katie admits she didn't understand the anguish her husband must have felt from losing the business and not being able to provide support for his children until she experienced a similar incident in her life. "When I saw my husband take over all our expenses, including those relating to my three boys, I realized how meaningful sharing financial responsibilities was in a relationship."

Use the Rough Time to Enhance Rather Than Destroy Your Relationship

Success during these times depends on the depth of your commitment to each other. It also depends on a daily dash of fun and creativity. Make room during the glum times for romantic walks, relaxing massages and dancing in your living room late at night. Use the expected times of dotage—birthdays, anniversaries, and Christmas or Hanukkah—to give a gift of love your spouse will never forget. Years later, we fondly remember and proudly use the button box, paperweight or napkin holder our children made for us. If the "make me something" concept works so well with children who have no appreciable spending money, why shouldn't it work as well with adults—on a more sophisticated level? Let me share with you a few of the most wonderful gifts I and others have ever given or received:

- To my husband, a crossword puzzle enthusiast, his own personal crossword puzzles that I developed using clues that only the two of us would know.
- To me, a month of Saturdays from my husband, to be used for me to do anything I wanted (or nothing at all), when he would cheerfully take over all the household chores from shopping to carpooling, cleaning to cooking.
- To each other, because both of them had always wanted middle names, Adele and Milton exchanged initials. He became Milton A. and she became Adele M. On their anniversary they signed the papers that forever linked them and altered their legal names.

I wouldn't want to end this chapter romanticizing the times of trouble, for they're difficult and consuming. They *can* destroy relationships, but they can also solidify them. "If we could get through those early years, we can get through anything," my husband reminds me.

Chapter Seven

The "Ours" Child

Maybe it's been a while since you've brought a new baby into this world. Maybe the experience is new. In either case, a bird's eye view of the costs might be in order.

Merely getting outfitted for this baby can cost as much as $7,000 (or more) the first year for furniture, clothes, toys and other equipment. Today, just to seat babies, we have body slings, car seats (in different sizes), infant seats, high chairs, umbrella strollers, jogging strollers—and a whole array of double-duty contraptions. Since well over half of mothers with children under the age of six works, day care expenses need to be included in the first year's costs. They're substantial.

And we can expect a child's costs to continue to increase.

A family with average earnings of $75,000 can expect to spend more than $375,000 to feed, clothe and shelter little Sally until she's 18 (not including college). That's just the beginning. If you want to send her to private or parochial school, give her piano, tennis, skiing or karate lessons, or stash money away for college tuition, magnify the basic figure. And there are other financial realities to contend with:

- Other children in the family are depending on us for economic security.
- The cost of higher education has outpaced inflation—and probably will continue to do so.
- In the future, our homes will probably appreciate a slower, saner rate than in the past, which means we will have less equity to tap into.

- Because we may be having this child later in our lives, there's a good chance her college years will butt up against our retirement years—doubling the pressure of "low income-high expenses" times.

All that being said, children are blessings, not assets. They can't be evaluated using formulas or by financial worth. And in a remarriage there is considerable evidence that the "ours" child can enrich the stepfamily. In the conclusion of her book, *Yours, Mine, and Ours: How Families Change When Remarried Parents Have A Child Together*, Anne Bernstein talks about her own experiences and those of the people she interviewed. "What emerges from the variety and complexity of the interviews is a portrait of stepfamily life that, while not without blemish, becomes more dimensional and vibrant when it includes at least 'one that's ours.'"

A MEETING OF THE MINDS

Deciding to have an "ours" child might be one of the most difficult decisions you'll have to face. Not everyone who remarries wants one. I did—even though I had three and my husband had five. My husband didn't. When the reality and enormity of our joint responsibilities touched every dollar and emotion we had, which happened within the first month of marriage, I changed my mind. Eight was enough.

Other people come to different conclusions. To a large degree, the number of children a woman has had before remarriage will influence the decision whether to have another. Understandably, women with two or more children are significantly less likely to have additional children in a second marriage. So, too, with men. But since most men choose to remarry women who are younger than their first wives, it's more likely that the partner without children will be the woman.

The decision to have or not have an "ours" child becomes part of the marriage negotiations, says psychologist Bernstein. That was what happened when Stuart and Carole began discussing the subject. Stuart had three children from a former marriage; Carole had no children and had never been married before.

"At first Stuart said 'yes,' he wanted more children," Carole says. "And that was important to me. I came from a large, loving family and wanted at least one of my own. As his children became heavier and heavier financial drains on our resources, Stuart changed his mind. It was a difficult time in our marriage," Carole recalls. "His unilateral decision prompted a sense of desolation in me. I was so depressed that I went to see a therapist. With her help, I was able to articulate my desires and my needs to him."

Our relationship had gotten to the point that we were going in opposite directions," Stuart says. "I didn't want that. One Sunday I went to church—something I hadn't done for years. Strangely, and I do mean strangely because I'm not a religious person, I had a vision of a bird coming down and putting his wings around me and saying that everything would be all right. I took that as a sign that if we had a child together, we would be able to handle it."

They now have one daughter and one son, ages three and one. Carole works part time as a physical therapist in a Boston suburb. Stuart has a solid managerial position and earns enough to cover the additional expenses.

"If any decision was made based on an act of faith," Stuart laughs, "having our children was."

Ages and number of other children in the family, ages of husband and wife, attitudes of both partners about parenthood, where each partner is in the life cycle, how strongly one of them wants a child—all these are considerations when making a decision whether to have a child of your own.

So, too, are the financial questions, such as how you will replace the loss of income if one parent stays home with new baby or only works part time.

Jancey and Ralph have a problem. They (but most vociferously, she) would like to have a child together. She would like to stay home with this child, something she wasn't able to do with her son from a prior marriage. But Ralph's small advertising agency is struggling. Without the substantial income from her one-woman personnel agency, they couldn't live. ""Despite the fact that I fight tenaciously for my independence," Jancey admits, "I have an irrational side. It says, 'I'm a woman and my husband should take care of me.' Since Ralph is not able to be the sole support of the family now, I'd rather wait to have the child—even though, at 41, I don't have much time."

STEPS TO TAKE BEFORE OR WHEN "OURS" ARRIVES

Beef Up Your Emergency Fund

When baby no longer makes three—more like four or five or six—there can rarely be too much money in an emergency fund. You never know when you'll need to draw on money at a moment's notice. The rule-of-planning is to have three to six months' worth of living expenses readily available for an emergency. Since a woman frequently takes anywhere from three weeks to six months off from work after giving birth, fortify your money market fund or account reserves to cover at least four months' expenses. If you don't have the funds to transfer, stash the savings from a reduction in spending or from a cutback in contributions to other accounts, such as IRAs or retirement plans like 4-1(k)s.

Update and Increase Your Insurance

If you're an income producer, your income probably is needed to maintain the family's standard of living. The odds are far greater that you'll suffer a disability that will keep you away from work for more than three months than they are that you will die. Do you have adequate disability coverage to handle this possibility?

And life insurance. If your other children are beneficiaries of the policy, do you want to add this one as well? If your spouse is the beneficiary, do you want to increase the coverage so he or she will have more resources to cover this child's expenses in the even of your death?

Add this baby to you health coverage as well.

Claim an Extra Withholding Allowance
Because you'll be claiming an additional dependency exemption on your tax return, you'll be paying less in taxes (assuming a level income). By changing your W-4 form (which determines how much tax is withheld from your paycheck), you'll be boosting your take-home pay.

Start an Education Fund
Gift money from relatives can be used to see a college fund. You can buy U.S. Series EE Savings Bonds, which accumulate interest tax-free while you own them. If you cash them in during a year that you pay college tuition for the child, you might not be required to pay tax on the accumulated interest.

You might also consider buying tax-exempt bond funds or growth-oriented mutual funds are earmarked for your child's education. These let you keep control of the money, and in the case of tax-exempt funds, give you a tax break as well.

If you put assets in your child's name, you do so with a custodial account. The tax savings in transferring money to children have been reduced somewhat over the past years, but they still exist. Until your child reaches age fourteen, the first $500 of his or her investment income is tax-free. The next $500 is taxed at the child's rate (almost always a better rate than yours), and any additional earnings are taxed at your rate.

Revise Your Estate Plan

How you plan to have this child taken care of in case of your death depends on how much money is available and whether this is your only natural child. Says Atlanta estate attorney Ann Salo, "If this is a woman's first child, often she will expect her husband to provide for this child better than he does for his children from a former marriage."

You will want to reexamine your wills. First, you have to name a guardian for this child in the event that both of you die. This can be a problem. If there are other children living in your family home, presumably they will be cared for by your former spouse. That means your child will be shuttled off to a relative or friend while her half-siblings (to whom she might be very close) will go in another direction. Unless yours is an unusual setup, siblings will be separated.

For the parent whose only child is "ours," there are fewer questions about who, eventually, will be the heir. More estate planning challenges face the parent who has two or more sets of children.

There are a variety of solutions. Here are three:

Donna and Roy have two children together and Roy has three from a former marriage who live with their mother. "We split things among the kids to reflect the fact that if we both die, two out of five children would have lost both parents and three of five would have lost one," says Donna. "Roy and I split our property. One half is mine; one half his. My will gives my property to our two children. His is divided up five ways because he has five children. We each have life insurance naming each other as beneficiary. This arrangement feels fair to both of us.

Antoinette has two sons, one from a former marriage and one with her husband Phil. She has left her whole estate in trust for both children. For as long as he's alive, Phil has the right to all the interest from the trust and can even invade the principal if he needs it. On his death, the estate will be divided between Antoinette's children. Phil's plan is different. At the time of his death, half his estate will go to Antoinette directly and the other half will go into a trust that will benefit her during her lifetime, but upon her death will go the their son only.

Leslie and Edward have two daughters together. Edward also has a son from a previous marriage. "My son lives with his mother, who has inherited a few million dollars from her father, and his stepfather, a nice chap who's wealthy in his own right," says Edward. "I know my son will be well cared for by his mother, so I'm not going to worry about his sharing in my estate. That will go to my wife and daughters. But I don't want him to feel like I'm leaving him nothing, so I've taken out an insurance policy that names him as beneficiary and leaves him a token amount of money."

How do you divide your estate among children in their early twenties and a young child? A young child must be thought of in a different context," affirms New York matrimonial attorney Jacalyn Barnett. "He or she needs more than a twenty-year-old who already has been supplied with many things. So though leaving unequal amounts to different children may appear unfair if the numbers are placed alongside each other, I don't think it necessarily is." A trust that allows the trustee to distribute (or sprinkle) funds to children where and when they are needed, such as for the care and education of the younger children, can be established to handle the looming needs of the younger children. Eventually when the younger children are grown, whatever is left of the legacy can be divided equally among all the children.

Because teenagers and adult children can interpret the inequality of the bequests as an inequality of love, you do best to explain the rationale of your decisions to those children old enough to understand and those who might feel slighted by the apportionment. Remember, too, that money isn't everything. More precious to many are the heirlooms and family mementos, which should be given or bequeathed to those for whom they would have the most meaning.

HOW "OURS" AFFECTS FAMILY FINANCES

Unless you're able to increase the size of the financially pie or the pie is unusually large, having another child will affect the resources available to other children in the family. There might be less for "his" and "hers." But that's the way it would be in any family. More financial responsibility means more sharing.

Parents have to stay alert to the fact that teenagers sometimes see the little intruder as putting a hand directly in their pockets, even when that's not the case.

"I thought my mother and stepfather would ante up for a car this year because most of my friends' parents did. But then the baby came and they said 'no,' " Robert recounts. It took scores of hours of arguing and then explaining for Robert to understand that the turndown wasn't linked to the baby. "They don't think a sixteen-year-old should have a car of his own," Roberts explains. "They have said that if I decide I want a car in two years and work to save the money for it, they'll provide me with matching funds. I'm surprised and annoyed because I assumed something so different. But I have to admit they're not mean. It's just that we'd never talked about this before."   The excitement of a pregnancy and the chaos of establishing a family life worked against solid communication in Robert's family. His parents had never found out what Robert was thinking—and he made the mistake of assuming they knew.

Having a baby together blurs the financial separateness of most remarriages. Not that husbands and wives are going to abandon their individual accounts. They might not. But the joint account, which might have been slim before (or never established), will swell. "Ours" children are cradled in "our" money. And that commitment to joint spending and joint funds spills over into the whole extended family.

It wasn't until our daughter was born that I began to understand why Jack was so generous to his children," Eleanor says. *"Even though I still catch myself in a why-is-he-buying-them-the best-sled-for-Christmas mode once in while, I can appreciate—for the most part—why he spends what he does. In fact, now I'm the one who urges that we buy his children more."*

Although there are no hard statistics to bear this out, observers conclude that, in many instances, "ours" children provide the stepchildren with a rallying point and give weight to the remarried couple's commitment to an enduring relationship.

Chapter Eight

Financial Links:
They Extend from Former
Spouse to Stepchildren
...and Beyond

Remarriage is its own special entity. It can't be, shouldn't be, and doesn't work if it's a facsimile of a first marriage. When you remarry, you create a real family, but it's unique because of its complexity and because the financial links often are as extended as the number of people you are or were related to. For every complicated financial arrangement with a member of the extended family, a myriad of creative solutions exists. To uncover them you have to come to terms with a new reality, invent traditions, and unrein your imagination.

In the best of all possible worlds, you and your present family would have enough money to live comfortably; your former spouses and children from former marriages would have the same. No jealousy or vindictiveness would mar the general well-being and spirit of cooperation of all the loosely linked families. But that's rarely the case. Some children wind up with more, some with less. Some families barely scrape by; others prosper.

Former family members can stay financially linked for many years and through subsequent marriages. Many will agree with Paul, who says that's too long. "I thought that because we never had children and I have remarried, we'd never have anything to do with one another again," he says of his first wife. "That's not the way it is, though. Her attorney calls mine once a year—like clockwork—seeking more spousal support."

And when there are children from a former marriage, the financial ties string out over years. The remarried challenge is to fulfill financial obligations to former families as you build a financial base with your new family. If the ideas offered here don't fit your situation, build on them to create your own solutions.

FINANCIAL LINKS WITH FORMER SPOUSES

Alimony or Spousal Support

When the vitriol between spouses still surges, writing an alimony check can be stressful. The deed must be done, no debate about that. But how? One easy way is to have your bank automatically transfer money out of your account each month to pay your obligation.

Another option is to ask your new spouse to write the check from your account or from your joint account (however you decide). Don't have your spouse sign the check; that has a way of infuriating the former spouse. You sign it. Make sure that check is tucked in among other checks requiring your signature so that you can pass over quickly and it won't evoke strong passion. Don't be surprised, however, if the residual of rancor seeps in when your wife makes out the check. Says Alaine, "I write it out and it's always on time. But my little 'noogie" is to put the return address sticker that has my name, not Peter's, on the envelope."

The most positive approach, and a good long-range solution to the alimony angst, is talk yourself into another frame of mind when writing the check. Instead of focusing on the money that your "rotten, conniving" former spouse is getting, interpret the act of writing the check as evidence of what a responsible person you are.

Child Custody Changes

At the time of a remarriage (and in the early years thereafter), many children move from one parent's household to the other's. Sometimes it's because one parent has remarried into a more financially comfortable situation and can provide children with a more stable and secure household.

"Nathan, the youngest of three children (the older two were girls), had a problem fitting into the family from the time he was a baby. He was hyperactive and not as verbal or sharp as his powerful older sisters," says John, Nathan's father. "Living with my ex— a threatening sort of person herself— was destroying his self-image entirely. When I remarried a woman who had a son Nathan's age—who Nathan looked up to—we decided it would be better if he lived with us instead of with his mother. Even though his mother demanded money to make the change of custody legal at first, she relented because this was a good deal for her. She couldn't handle him—or was inept at it—anyway."

Other times, a child moves into a different household because he or she can't get along with the new stepparent.

"Audrey was eleven when Alan and I married,' says Laura, a computer analyst from Roanoke. "It was difficult for her for a number of reasons. She and I had become so close in the eight years we had lived together that she considered Alan an intruder. And he was, in a way. He wanted to spend time with me alone (and I wanted time with him, too) and he wasn't subtle about excluding Audrey from dinners out, for example. Audrey became so nasty to him that it was intolerable. And Alan, who hadn't lived with children since his divorce eleven years ago, didn't know how to talk to her. Sometimes he would act as if he wanted nothing to do with her. Other times he'd try to be nice and supportive. And at other times he'd order her around.

"As much as I tried to mediate their growing feuds, nothing helped. Not even family therapy, which we tried for about four months. On the sly, Audrey

spoke to her father, who she wasn't particularly close to, and asked to live with him, his wife, and their two children. He suggested that they try it for a year."

Laura admits she was devastated by the turn of events. But she agreed, simply to try to cool down a difficult situation.

Ten months later, at the end of the school year, Audrey asked to come back to Laura and Alan's house. "This time Alan is making a real effort to stabilize the family," Laura said, "because he realizes how important it is to me and how much I was hurting when Audrey was away. And Audrey, too, is trying not to be so belligerent to Alan. I don't know exactly why, but my guess is that her life wasn't as rosy in her father's household as she thought it would be."

Court Actions

When child custody changes, it is often done through a court order (although some parents, those who can still talk civilly to each other, can make their new arrangements informally).

There are other reasons for court actions. Nothing prevents a former spouse from suing for more money for support. And in doing so, most courts allow full discovery of the new spouse's income and assets. Stepparents are not legally required to support stepchildren under most circumstances. Still, if you marry someone with a wonderfully lucrative career and you live well from her income, for example, your former spouse might be able to convince the court that you can afford to pay more child support, even though your income may still be the same or even lower than when you signed the separation agreement.

And, of course, nothing prevents a former spouse from suing to enforce some unimportant violation in a separation agreement (such as your not sending, annually, copy of a life insurance policy with him or her named as beneficiary). It can be shattering to a remarriage to have a former spouse intrude by subpoena. Pile the emotional damage onto the financial—having to pay lawyers megabucks to defend yourself on frivolous charges— and you have a nasty situation. Some courts, clogged with important family matters, have no patience or time for what they consider nuisance suits, and, after a number of such, stipulate there will be sanctions assessed against the party losing the suit. Often the sanctions include paying the winning attorney's fees (in addition to one's own attorney, of course) and all court costs. In an effort to discourage lawyers from taking on these suits, some courts also order the losing attorney to pay a penalty.

The Stepfamily Association of America reports that it gets calls from people (mainly fathers) who are being sued either by their former wives or by children from a former marriage for educational expenses (or part of them), even though nothing is written into a separation agreement. In general, plaintiffs (former spouses and children) have a difficult time winning because there's no real logic for this kind of suit. No law exists that requires a parent who hasn't been divorced to provide higher education expenses for children.

Money Messengers

Don't saddle children with relaying money messages to a former spouse, and don't allow your former spouse to do it either. When a child comes to you with a request from the other parent for more money, don't get sucked into discussing it with the child. Insist that money discussions remain between you and the other parent. You're relieving the child of the onerous burden of acting as a go-between—a position children should never be in.

As for whether to meet the requests for additional support, that's a decision you have to make. If you can afford it and the request seems reasonable, then you might choose to do so. If you can't afford it, you might refuse.

Financial Decisions Concerning Children

The person who pays has more influence over decisions. That may not be fair, but it's reality. But what do you do when both biological parents contribute to children's support and feel keenly about their welfare but are at loggerheads over some monetary decision? For example, what if you don't agree on whether your child should go to private school? Or if you both subscribe to the concept that he should but can't agree on which one would be best?

To move beyond the sparks-flying stage, consider working with a third party—someone trained in techniques of family mediation. In a bit of a twist, one that can be successful only if there is an amicable relationship between the nuclear and the stepfamily, In one family, Natalie, the stepmother, serves as mediator. "I think it works because both parents and the children see me as the objective third party—and because both parents honestly try to make decisions that are in the best interests of their children. And," she admits, "it certainly helps that I have no children of my own, and that we have enough money so that no one feels deprived."

Keep in mind that solutions to problems take negotiation, compromise, persistence, and time.

You Can't Pay What You Owe to a Former Spouse

It happens. Even when you have the best of intentions, a business fails, a family member needs money for a serious medical problem, the value of investments set aside for the children's education plummets—and the funds that had been promised are not available as planned. You have five choices.

1. Immediately file an order with the court to modify your support payments. "That stops a lot of nasty things from happening," says matrimonial lawyer Randy Kaplan. "You can't be held in contempt for not paying (or not paying the full amount), which means you won't be thrown into jail. Courts recognize that on occasion people are not able to meet their financial obligations. If you can show a substantial change of circumstances, the court might grant a reduction (or temporary reduction) in support payments. And you don't need an attorney

to file for a modification. You can go to court and file the papers yourself." (That's important to know, especially when you're in financial straits.)

2. Assuming your former spouse is amenable, you can work with each other or through a third party to mediate a resolution. Rodney, who has a separation agreement that calls for half the tuition of a state college be borne by each parent, didn't have the money when his daughter was ready for school. "So my former wife and I agreed that she'd pay it," he explained, "and when she sells the house she and my children are living in, she will take the tuition money out of my share."

   Joyce, another financially squeezed parent who was unable to provide college funds she thought she'd have by the time her son was ready for college, made a verbal commitment to him and to his custodial father. He was to apply for financial aid. When he graduated, she would help him pay back the loan. That proved to be an acceptable arrangement.

3. You can look for the money elsewhere. Parents, relatives, banks, or new spouses are possible sources. As a loan, this approach works only if there is a reasonable prospect you'll be able to repay it and the loan source subscribes to the deal—financially and emotionally. One new spouse was delighted to come to the aid of her husband, whose business was in a slump. "As long as I have the extra money," she said, "I have no problem using it toward my stepson's tuition." In that case, they money was given as a gift.

4. You might get sued (if you're the debtor) or institute suit (if you're the person to whom money is owed.

5. You can resign yourself to not getting the money. Or, if you're the one reneging, resign yourself to the consequences of being delinquent, which often include the wrath of children as well as of a former spouse.

Children as Ragamuffins

You provide your former spouse with what you consider a sizable support check each month, yet when the children come visiting each summer, they're in tatters. You and your spouse wind up buying them everything from toothbrushes to swimsuits to underwear. It galls you.

Forget the fleeting thought that you'll subtract the amount spend from the next support check. That's not on the up-and-up. Those items that might be used each visit—toothbrush, comb, beach towels, oversized sweatshirts—can be kept at your home for future visits. Those items the children will outgrow from visit to visit should be packed in the suitcases when they return home. Anything less is petty.

Children's Weddings

The guiding rule during these high-stress times, according to stepfamily experts John and Emily Visher, is that everyone concerned should concentrate on how the young person would like this affair to go and not on "evening the score" or resolving old issues between households. These precepts hold true no matter who pays.

Unless the young person has no relationship with the other biological parent, the nonpaying parent and his or her spouse should be invited, as well as the young person's close relatives on that side of the family. Beyond that, there are personal choices. Is the invited parent asked to contribute for his or her invitees? Does the nonpaying parent play a dominant role in the wedding planning and ceremony? Who pays for the prenuptial dinner? For the wedding attire of attendants (especially if they're members of another household)?

No universal answer exists for any of these questions, but the litmus test answer for all of them rests with the young person getting married: What is his or her preference? If it can be accommodated, then that is the solution.

Alternatives to traditional large weddings work well when there are problems between two households. Small weddings in the offices of a clergyperson or a judge or on board a boat (performed by an authorized ship's captain) can be memorable. Before or after the actual ceremony, families can host parties, jointly or separately, honoring the young couple.

ONE FAMILY LINKED TO ANOTHER

Even if they are hundreds of miles apart, former families and new families seem to know exactly how the other is living—and it's usually extravagantly, according to reports and rumor.

"I know they are spending thousands on renovation and going away on lavish vacations," said Marge, even though she admitted that these conclusions were based on bits and pieces of information from her five-year-old son, Kevin, after he came home from a two-week stay at his father and stepmother's house. "And we never go anywhere."

Stepmother Judy as astounded when she learned of what Marge was saying. "We're always scrimping. Marge and her husband are the wealthy ones. They have two cars—one a Mercedes. And they went on a lovely holiday while Kevin was visiting us."

Whatever side of the financial line you're on, it seems like the wrong side. This is true especially with children, who because of their lack of sophistication and confusion over the remarriage configuration, assume that the kids living in the "other" house are getting more.

Telling Children about the Family's Finances
For those remarrieds bringing children from a former marriage into the fold, there is always the question of what children should be told about the couple's new financial picture. That's true in biologically intact families too, but in remarriages the questions are more complicated because there are more people involved. Also, most remarrieds aren't anxious to

give children information about their finances that their children will later share with a former spouse.

Much of the decision about what to tell and what not to tell, of course, depends on the age and maturity of the children, as well as how comfortable the adults (all of them—parents and stepparents) are in discussing the situation.

Given the swirling changes that remarriage brings to children, parents have to try to keep money and financial problems from creating more stress for them. Money talks can become a vehicle to further unity, if by words and deed they can assure the children of the couple's commitment to each other and to each other's children. Without drawing children into the fray with former spouses, parents and stepparents have to be able to explain problems as unemotionally as possible in ways that do not make the children feel they are the cause of the plight or responsible for finding the solutions to financial issues. In some cases where the children are old enough to understand, it makes sense to explain, where they're involved, the terms of separation agreement signed with a former spouse.

"My kids were pissed off at me because their mother told them she wasn't getting alimony," Barney relays. *"What she didn't tell them was the reason for that. I've had a heart condition for many years. When we were divorced, we decided she should have the house and 90 percent of our savings because I can't be sure of how long I'll be working. This way she and children won't have to count on my being healthy for their daily bread. When they understood the reasons behind the agreement, our relations improved, and they didn't think I was stiffing them anymore."*

Phone Calls
Rarely does the phone bill between former spouses become excessive. They are usually all too happy to keep their conversations brief.

It's those long distance calls made by your children or stepchildren to their noncustodial parent that can be astronomical. To add insult to injury, you suspect the children are pouring out their unhappiness with you new marriage and it galls you to have to pay for it.

No matter how well it seems to be going, remarriage is difficult and confusing for children. They face divided loyalties and resent any attempt you make to limit contact with the noncustodial parent. On the other hand, you can't give them free rein to run up excessive phone bills. You have a number of options or combination of options.

- Make certain you are using the long distance service that best suits your particular situation. All major companies have their own supersaver programs designed for frequent long distance users.

- Noncustodial parents can get a personal 800 number. Then children can call them whenever they want and talk for as long as they want, and the cost will be on the other parent's proverbial dime.

- Set limits on the length of calls to the parent, but make the limits realistic. If the children need to talk beyond that, ask them to have the parent call back.

- If the children are teens—which means the phone is probably a problem anyway—consider installing a separate phone line for them. You can tell them you'll pay for up to X dollars each month and they're responsible for the rest from money they earn. Teens like the privacy of their own lines. Having them contribute to the bill is a valuable money management lesson.

Kids Play the Fairness Issue

Get used to it. Until children are old enough and have had enough distance from the emotional upheavals of divorce and remarriage to assess the situation objectively, the grass on the other family's lawn will not only be greener, it will be more expensive as well. They will see inequities—real or imagined—and, often without realizing what they're doing, will play on the initial confusion (at perhaps guilt) associated with the remarriage to put the squeeze on parents for a new toy, bike or car. And parents are easy targets—especially Disneyland Dads, those fathers whose children are treated to whirlwind spending when they visit. The fathers (and in some cases mothers) feel guilty about not being a full-time presence in their children's lives, so they try to make up for it with things and amusements. Especially when money is tight, this extraordinary treatment rankles other members of the new family. Expensive entertainment, writes Marcella Sabo in *Whose Kid Is It Anyway*, "could certainly create worry for a wife and cause her to feel a sense of inadequacy regarding what she can provide for her own children." The option: more talk, games, and at-home activities, which allow for a natural interaction between parent and visiting child.

We parents shouldn't get caught in the "she got something I didn't get" competition that children are especially adept at playing—whether they're stepsiblings or siblings of a nuclear family. They want us to equate fairness with equality, which, of course, is not accurate. In actuality, equality warps fairness. Would it be fair to give your six-year-old son and twelve-year-old stepson the same allowance? Or deprive a musically gifted child of violin lessons simply because her stepsiblings are not talented? Would you go out on an equal financial limb to support two children in college—one who pulls all-nighters in the library and the other who's out all night in bars? "Being relentlessly equal negates the connection between money and need, which is the real issue when it comes to financial fairness," says Claire Berman, author of *Making It as a Stepparent*.

While a grand display of unequal gift-giving is inappropriate, the value of a present should not be measured by how much is spent on it. The best way to give a gift is to concentrate on its meaning, not its cost. A DVC player for a music enthusiast, an outfit for a teenager, or a whistles and bells bike for a pre-schooler may not be equal in price, but in the eyes of the receiver each is special and valued.

Kids are masters at pressuring or manipulating parents with the "You're not fair" taunt. When they're in their teens, nettlesome sullenness or freshness replaces the childish challenge. Instead of caving in to some perceived guilt, we, as adults, have to be clear about what we can spend—and then explain it to our children.

Josh and Ginny admit they've spent many an evening holed up on their bed grappling with the fact that one child is going to private college and the other will not. "But we finally got together on it," Ginny says, "and are presenting a united front. Going to a private college isn't an inalienable right."

Says Josh: "My stepdaughter Laura drives a used BMW that Ginny and I bought for her when she turned sixteen. Now she's eighteen and wants to go to the University of Pennsylvania like my son did. But that was eleven years ago, and college costs have risen dramatically—more than our income, I might add. We can afford the tuition for the state university, but my feeling is that if Laura wants to go to Penn, she should contribute something—perhaps by selling her car and using that money. She now accuses us of being unfair. 'What has my car got to do with going to Penn?' she asks. Thank heavens Ginny and I talked this out beforehand, because I really care for Laura and don't want to come out the heavy on this issue by leading Ginny or Laura to believe I'm playing favorites."

"Sure I want to help all our children with their college educations," says Joe, a Detroit-based computer sales representative. "And they know that. But I've also told them that while my son didn't have to work which he was in school because his grandparents covered most of the costs, Julie's twins, my stepdaughters, will. They don't have the same financial reservoir. They'll get some money from us, but not enough to cover all their expenses. You could say that it's not fair—especially since the girls are better students than my son is. But life isn't always fair. Nor is fairness the issue here. This is a monetary decision."

The fact that one set of biological grandparents are wealthy and eager to assume some responsibility for their grandchild's education further emphasizes the unevenness of the playing field—not unusual in remarriages.

Husband and wife come to the new union with varying assets—some personal, some familial. They've had more time and opportunity to build both assets and debts than they had in a first marriage. So have their families. And if there's a noncustodial parent providing additional support, that's another imbalance.

Among the most important factors in determining who gets what among stepsiblings are the ages and needs of the children. Resources will be mobilized for a ten-year-old with a serious medical problem that will not be available to the eighteen-year-old who would like a car, for example.

Differing Attitudes

In remarriages, spouses often bring very disparate ideas about money to the marriage. For example, William feels that, as a matter of principle, children should be responsible for their own college education. His wife, Elsie, on the other hand, thinks it's her duty to make certain her children's every educational need is met. She's willing to work two jobs to ensure that. So, depending on how committed William's children are to furthering their education, it may be that Elsie's children will go to college immediately after high school and William's won't.

Living With Imbalance

Laurie and Michael have the classic stepfamily inequity situation—one that there's very little control over. Laurie explains it.

"I'm in the second year of a three-year master's degree program in social work so I'm not earning anything now. My husband Michael is a drug rehabilitation counselor at a clinic. His salary, plus interest from an inheritance from his mother, is just enough to support our baby daughter and us. My former husband, Patrick, and I have joint custody of our two teenage boys, which means the boys are with Michael and me four days a week and with Patrick for three. Although Patrick pays for the boys' clothes and allowances, we cover whatever it costs for them when they're with us—food, school lunch money and

the like. By separation agreement, I'm also expected to contribute a monthly sum to a fund that is to take care of the boys' educational and recreational expenses. But I've been unable to do that since I gave birth.

"The problem is that Patrick, who is a major executive with a large drug firm, makes more than he can spend and has no other financial responsibilities. So there's a real difference in what the boys can do and get in the two households."

Laurie says that though the children have adjusted to some of the restrictions imposed by her current economic situation, they continue to press for certain amenities, like phones of their own which they enjoy at one home but not the other.

"I find myself caught between the desire to please the boys and the need to pay attention to economic realities," she says. "And don't think the boys don't occasionally try to exploit my guilt at having wanted the divorce and putting them in this situation in the first place."

The issue is further tested because Michael is pressing Laurie to sue Patrick for child support. "Even if it was $100 a week, it would help," Michael says. "It's only fair if he wants the boys to be happy." Laurie is unwilling to petition the court.

Yes, there's considerable financial disparity between Laurie and Michael's household and Patrick's. The question, however, is "Is it unfair?" And if so, to whom? To Laurie? To Michael? To the boys?

Unless the deprivation at Laurie and Michael's is extreme and the boys go hungry when they're there (which isn't the case), fairness isn't the paramount issue. Laurie and Michael have to explain to the boys, in as much detail as possible, how the two households differ—excising from the discussion and tone of their voices the resentment and anger they now feel. The subtle life lessons that money isn't everything, that fairness doesn't equal sameness or happiness, will eventually be learned. In the long run, it's more important for Laurie and Michael to accept the temporary financial strain than to worry about parity between the households or feel guilty that it doesn't exist.

The reality is that money does tie two households together. Unless both households operated independently of each other financially, any disparity between former spouses can become a thorny issue or a way to bully decisions in favor of the moneyed parent.

Disparity not only affects the former spouses; it drags in the new spouses as well. Indeed, writes Patricia Lowe in *The Cruel Stepmother*, "Unless all concerned have plenty of money, it may and probably will influence the climate between the divorced parents and their offspring through the growing-up period. It touches decisions about education, housing, clothing, vacations, the medical and dental services chosen, and a whole raft of other problems sticky enough in their own right."

Financial strains as a result of money paid to a former household can have a dramatic influence on a remarriage, especially in the early years.

LINKS BETWEEN STEPPARENTS AND STEPCHILDREN

Stepparents often have strong emotional bonds to their stepchildren. So despite what the law says about their financial obligations, they're often eager to help with part or all of the children's financial support—acting as if they were the biological parent.

Legal Responsibility for Children
The law differs from state to state, but generally, you as a stepparent are not legally responsible for children who don't live with you.

What about those who do? Primary financial responsibility lies with the biological parents. But suppose you're the stepfather and the child's biological father has disappeared or died, and your wife has very little money of her own. To avoid the possibility of the child becoming a public charge, most states hold to the position that you, the stepfather, must assume some financial responsibility.

As long as they can afford it, providing necessities doesn't bother most stepparents. The troubling aspects of financial support are subtler. Do you provide money for a car after you stepchild's biological parent refuses? Do you help with medical school tuition because you care about this child and don't want her saddled with debt when she graduates? Do you make certain that your stepson has the same access to college funds that your own son has? These are personal questions with personal answers.

Money to Stepchildren

By the time you and child have lived together for a number of years, you have a fair handle on what type of person he or she is. For some kids, asking for money is very difficult. They feel childish, humiliated, or generally uncomfortable about being on the receiving end of the transaction. For others, money is an entitlement, due them simply because they're here on earth and ask for it.

"When do I say 'no' and when do I say 'yes' to requests for money?" asks one stepmother of three teenagers, who, because she has no children of her own, is inexperienced in this area.

There are good reasons to say no:

- You can't afford it.
- You'd like to help out in another way. In the case of college tuition, for example, offer to work on the financial aid form with the young person, or suggest various sources for grants and scholarships.
- You think the request is irresponsible. Money for the teen's car (he's wrecked two already) is not high on your priority list.

- You don't like the young person, and he or she doesn't like you. Stepchild or not, you still have the right to refuse money to someone for personal reasons.
- You think you can buy the child's love. "If I get the concert tickets for her, she'll finally talk to me." But that won't be the case. She's not going to stop being hard as nails because you're a soft touch. Her hostility will continue because she knows now she can get what she wants from you, civil or not.

There are good reasons to say yes:
- You can afford it.
- It's a source of personal pleasure to help out someone you care about.
- The request is reasonable.

Chances are that the longer you and your stepchildren live together and know one another, the closer you will become and the more likely it will be that you will want to help out financially.

Financial Aid for Higher Education

Comprehensive financial aid forms ask for financial information from the parent the child lived with for most of the past twelve months. And despite the fact that the stepparent has no legal financial responsibility for his stepchild, the evaluation of aid will be based on the parent and stepparent's combined incomes and assets—even if some of the assets are owned separately. It makes no sense to exclude the other biological parent's finances on this form, but that's the way it is. The information is reported to each school your child applies to.

Because colleges realize the picture painted in the comprehensive form is not always accurate (and in the case of stepfamilies, it rarely is), they almost always will provide their own separate financial aid applications.

Here's an opportunity to tell all, including what your former spouse has agreed to pay, where he or she lives (complete with home and business phone numbers).

Expensive colleges are more likely to require information and money from the other biological parent than state or public schools. Rarely, however, do they get into the collection game. If a man, for example, refuses to honor a separation agreement made with his former wife that calls for a $10,000 a year contribution toward each child's college education, it is the wife, not the college, who will have to bring suit to collect it if it's not forthcoming.

But even if the father does pay, the sum will not normally reduce the contribution expected from the mother and stepfather. Sorry to say, but most colleges simply reduce your child's aid package by the amount provided by the noncustodial parent. And usually the reduction comes from the "free" money portion of the package—money that doesn't have to be repaid, like grants.

Sometimes a couple is in a position to and wants to help all the children (his, hers and theirs) with college expenses. One fair way of divvying up the pot is to calculate what each child will need and set up one savings (or investment) account. Each spouse contributes to the fund, even if the amounts differ substantially, and together they parcel out the money to each child based on need and the size of the fund.

Legal Rights of Stepparents

While many stepparents provide full financial support for their stepchildren, they have few legal rights. Actually, a biological parent who deserts the children has greater legal rights to them than the stepparent who rears and educates the kids.

Stepparents, for example, have no legal right to authorize medical treatment for their stepchildren, even though they may be acting as a parent. If the school or camp your child goes to doesn't have a form that include spaces for the names and contact information of stepparents, the

Stepfamily Association of America suggest that the spouse who's the biological parent in the household draft several identical letters, like the one that follows. Have each notarized and keep one on file at home and one on file at school or summer camp.

Sample Form

I, _____
Name of biological parent

_____, of
Indicate whether father or mother of child

_____
Name of child

Whose birthday is _____
Date

Hereby allow _____ to secure
Name of stepparent

medical attention/treatment/tests on behalf of my child.

_____
Signature of biological/custodial parent

Notary Public Validation

Stepparents and their spouses must be vocal in addressing the legal issues surrounding the recognition of stepparent involvement in families so that the new family structures are acknowledged and understood.

Adoption

Like marriage, the legal rite of adoption has a subtle, but profound, "connected" effect on a family. Also like marriage, it shouldn't be entered into lightly. From the stepparent's view, it's a financial obligation that extends beyond the marriage. If a couple gets divorced, the adoptive stepparent is as responsible for the child's support as if he or she were the biological parent.

Because the process of adopting a stepchild whose biological parent is still alive is formidable, most adoptions involve stepparents who are married to widows or widowers. In instances where there's a living parent, he or she must agree to surrender all parental rights. If the biological parent doesn't object, adoption is a simple process, with none of the formality of a regular adoption. There's no need for the nonbiological parent to go through a screening or approval process. If the noncustodial parent can't be found or if he or she refuses to concede the rights, however, the adoption can't be consummated.

Carefully consider the child's position in these proceedings. He or she might not want to be adopted, especially if it's proposed within a few years of the death of a biological parent. Children also have problems with name changes, so you might consider using his or her present last name as a middle name and hyphenating it to the new name.

Custody Rights

"Stepparent custody" is almost an oxymoron. But there's hope. A large percentage of states have established legal rights of stepparents dealing with custody/visitation and support of minor children. And that's a good thing since so many stepchildren and stepparents develop tremendous love for one another and need to have visitation guaranteed by law.

ONE MORE LINK: STEPGRANDPARENTS

Unequal Gift-Giving

You can't force grandparents to spend the same amount on Christmas or Hanukkah presents for their stepgrandchildren as they do on their grandchildren. But you want to avoid a hurtful caste system that has one child beaming over a bike and the other brooding over a bookmark. Many grandparents are inept as stepgrandparents because their roles are new. They don't intend to be mean or thoughtless. To help them adjust to their new roles, remarried couples have developed some ingenious strategies to lighten the gift-giving occasions.

- They invent traditions, such as using a grab-bag approach to holiday gift-giving; allowing only homemade gifts during the holiday season; or giving gifts to charity instead of the family. Some families spend the holiday volunteering services at a hospital or for Meals on Wheels.

- One woman has her children make something for their stepgrandparents. Then, a few weeks before Christmas, she casually mentions to her in-laws how long and hard the kids have been working on this "surprise" gift. Knowing how much energy went into the "special" gift softens the reluctant grandparents' hearts and prompts them to reciprocate.

- Another woman talked to her in-laws about how lonely and strange her kids feel at holiday time and how they miss all the "old" faces at celebrations. The stepgrandparents understood because they, too, were feeling nostalgic for "what was." That was the impetus they needed to be more thoughtful with their stepgrandchildren.

FOOLPROOF MISTAKES

There are no solutions that work perfectly for all the financial links remarried families have to their members and to former families. But it's simple to spot what *won't* work. So here's a list of foolproof mistakes that you shouldn't practice.

1. *Maintain two completely different standards within the same stepfamily.*

    Why it doesn't work. Resident stepchildren and their parent can't help but feel offended when you play favorites or make no pretext about putting your own kids first. It's hard to be a family is everyone's entitlement is so different.

2. *Skimp on the new family, spend on the old.*

    Why it doesn't work. Even if you consider yourself the "family destroyer, the one who initiated the divorce in your former marriage, you're not going to ease your guilt or the pain of your former spouse and the children by "being there" for them with dollars.

    Money doesn't make up for the loss, and the inequity of the financial arrangement can cause resentment in the remarriage.

3. *Have relatives bestow lavish gift unequally.*

    Why it doesn't work. Encouraging your children's grandparents to make a big splash of the

    Honda Accord they're giving to your son for his sixteenth birthday and telling them it's fine to send your stepdaughter a card when she turns that "sweet" age, for example, is a resentment boiler. Of all the pressures of a remarriage, one of the most difficult to control involves wealthy, generous, loving grandparents or noncustodial parents indulging grandchildren or children in substantial gifts. When stepsiblings live together, the inequality of the giving is even more destructive. While it's presumptuous to tell another adult what to do with his or her money, we can encourage the generous relative to understand how the generosity breeds hostility. Perhaps the relative can be persuaded to make gifts less obvious or to divide the bounty more evenly.

4. *Rely too heavily on a former spouse.*

   Why it doesn't work. The financial ties that bind former spouses may choke the new marriage. Because money controls, the noncustodial parent who writes out hefty support checks can play all sorts of power games. He (and in most cases it's a he) can hold up the money because he doesn't want to send the child to private school or he can dawdle with payments just to be vindictive. If you're subject to a former spouse's whims and don't know when money will flow, both you and your new spouse will find yourselves focusing your energies and attention on your former spouse. He's in control. You wind up taking your eyes off the ball—forming your own financial union.

Remarried couples continuously have to reconfigure their funds to match the changing financial connections and obligations to immediate, extended, and former family members. Fortunately you're more knowledgeable about finances and more certain of your own financial philosophy that you were when you married for the first time. You're also less stuck in the "traditional" and more flexible about searching for creative solutions to new challenges. All of that works to your advantage when you find yourself financially linked to such a wide array of people.

Chapter Nine

Remarrying After the Children Are Grown

Dr. Carl Menninger was right. Love cures people—both the ones who give it and the ones who receive it. Research confirms that remarriage among people later in life is good for the body and good for the spirit. Yet remarriage after the death of or divorce from a long-term spouse raises new problems—many involving money. But because most money challenges have practical resolutions, it's absurd to allow money to stand in the way of less stress, greater self-esteem and more life satisfaction—all of which widows feel when they remarry.

If, as the joke goes, life begins after the children have gone to college and the dog dies, then remarriage at this age should be extraordinary. The problem is that by the time a person is old enough to have grown children, around fifty or fifty-five, there are 48 men to every 52 women. For women, the growing imbalance is made worse because men in their age group who do remarry frequently choose women considerably younger than themselves.

Other obstacles to remarriage between older adults include society's expectations following the death of a spouse. Bereavement customarily lasts a year; widows and widowers are advised not to rush into anything. The costs—financial and emotional—of marrying another partner who may become seriously ill also weigh heavily. Moreover, public policies sometimes work to your detriment when you remarry.

YOUR OWN CONCERNS

Martha, a sixty-eight-year-old wealthy widow whose deceased husband was president of a large textile company, is being told by her friends that the fifty-eight-year-old man courting her is interested only in her money.

Olga, a fifty-nine-year-old receptionist whose divorce left her with a small nest egg that she has stashed in bank CDs, fears that marrying anyone but a rich man will endanger her secure existence. So she's resisting the proposals of a sixty-three-year-old retired teacher whom she has been seeing for three years.

Edgar, a seventy-four-year-old retired production manager, is able to live with his woman friend comfortably on the pension and Social Security benefits he gets. He also has accumulated some savings and investments, which he's squirreled away to use only in case of health emergencies. Whatever's left he wants his son to inherit. He lives in a community property state and fears his longtime companion would get it all if they were to get married and he died first. So he's not proposing.

Vincent, a sixty-three-year old widower who's an executive with a major communications firm, can't seem to shake the fear that he'll be made a fool of if he marries a woman twelve years his junior. "I'm sure she's marrying me for my money, that she'll disappear shortly after we're married, and that the whole relationship will be a sham."

Remarriage provokes anxiety.

Both men and women question their readiness and their ability to make another commitment.

Older women, especially, worry about what they'll have to give up when they remarry. Will it be alimony (in the case of a divorce), career prospects (especially if a woman has been fending for herself successfully for quite a while and her new spouse is nearing retirement age), Social Security or pension benefits, or an adult child's emotional or financial support?

Still, many older women welcome the prospect of sharing life with a new spouse. They're eager for the companionship, sex, and financial interdependence. "I've noticed that even women who have been handling their finances alone for quite a while are inclined to abdicate the responsibility when they remarry," says Chicago financial planner Susan Richards. "Many women, especially those who were married before the feminist movement, feel that making money decisions is like changing the oil in your car. You might know how to do it, but who wants to?"

THERE'S A LOT TO TALK ABOUT

The prenuptial process, that of sharing financial information, anxieties, goals and dreams, is the same at sixty as it is at thirty. Only the subject matter changes. Now the concentration is on what you have in the way of assets, when, if ever, you want to retire, where you'd like to retire to, and what employee and retirement benefits you can expect. You also want to know each other's financial obligations to grandchildren or adult children and your current health status and prognosis. You'll want to discuss whether you'll buy or rent a new abode, move into one of your present homes, or move in with one of the children. You'll want to know how much insurance each of you has, who the beneficiaries are, and if the insurance is appropriate in type, cost and amount.

A Boston couple found their concerns about marriage needed to be addressed in a formal prenuptial agreement. They had known each other, off and on, for thirty years. When they lived in Boston, Mary Louise and her husband were friendly with Bob and his wife. Mary Louise and her husband moved to Virginia, and for a few years they kept in Christmas-card contact with Bob's family. Then correspondence faltered. A number of years later Mary Louise divorced. Then Bob divorced. It wasn't until Mary Louise came back to

Boston for her 35th high school reunion that she and Bob touched base again. By now Bob was confined to a wheelchair (though by no means inactive) as a result of multiple sclerosis. The genuine liking they had for one another many years ago turned into love. After a short courtship, they decided to get married. Mary Louise's kids expressed their concern about Bob's physical condition. "I told them this is life," Mary Louise said, "and life isn't a dress rehearsal. You've got to grab onto happiness when it's presented. Bob is funny, kind and exciting. I've been through too much to believe that life is an ice cream sundae that never melts. I'm going to dig in while I can."

Despite the fact that they both came into this marriage "with a commitment at least equal to that of my first marriage," says Bob, they both wanted a formal prenuptial agreement. "I was asking Mary Louise to be with me during some difficult times," Bob says. "We don't know how quickly this disease will progress. Even on days when I'm feeling well, she has to get me into my wheelchair. She's making sacrifices, and I wanted her to know that I appreciate them and that she'd always be taken care. At the same time, I want my pharmaceutical business to go to my children." All that was spelled out in a prenuptial agreement.

Mary Louise had her own reasons for wanting a prenuptial. They had to do with what she was giving up when she moved to Boston. She had a lovely home "that I couldn't replace here," a well paid job as a dental hygienists, and income from a babysitting service she had started. "It wasn't that I needed to be compensated for caring for someone I love," she says. "I just needed to feel financially secure if I was going to give up working."

FINANCIAL OBLIGATIONS WHEN THERE ARE HEALTH PROBLEMS

Sickness is always a possibility. Nobody likes to examine the prospect too closely, but the older you get, the more likely you are to have a close-up view of serious health problems—your own and your spouse's. What, you wonder silently, will happen to your financial resources if this new love of your life needs significant and extensive long-term medical care? Nobody wants to remarry and then, a few years later, find him or herself, stripped of all but a small portion of life savings as a result of a spouse's illness.

Obviously the chances of an extended nursing home stay are greater at seventy years of age than they are at thirty. So people remarrying later in life must address the possibility—and plan for it in the hope that the plans will never need to be executed.

As difficult as it is, talk about the whole health and finance issue prior to remarriage. With the help of estate planners and elderlaw attorneys who are savvy in Medicaid eligibility and coverage, you can make provisions for yourself and your new spouse that will minimize the erosion of assets in case long-term medical care is needed.

Peter Strauss, a New York attorney specializing in legal concerns of the elderly, outlines what people remarrying later in life might consider when they discuss finances and health:

1. Supplemental insurance planning to fill in the gaps in Medicare coverage.
2. HMO Medicare plans.
3. Long-term care insurance.
4. Medicaid planning, a form of estate planning that helps an at-home spouse remain solvent if his or her spouse needs nursing home care.
5. Language in a prenuptial agreement that *might* protect you from using your money to pay for nursing home care for a spouse.

Health Insurance Planning

While Medicare, the federal program that assists seniors and some disabled Americans with medical costs, will relieve you of some health-related expenses, there are gaps in the coverage. Private insurance companies have filled in some of the cracks with policies known as Medi-gap. But they're still confusing and have all sorts of rules governing coverage. The best way to decipher which is most appropriate for you is to carefully read the government's handbook, "Medicare & You" which is available by calling 1-800-MEDICARE (1-800-633-4227; TTY/TDD 1-877-486-2048 for the hearing and speech impaired; on the Net at *www.medicare.gov*).

Also consider HMO Medicare plans because they're sometimes less costly than Medicare and Medi-gap insurance. The problem is that they're also less reliable. Insurance companies have been cutting HMO Medicare coverage, raising premiums, or eliminating plans altogether, so be very cautious about switching to them.

Long-term-care insurance policies are definitely worth considering, because costs of nursing home care is so great. The majority of long-term policies pay a dollar amount per day for nursing home or home health care, but that's where the similarity among policies ends. At a minimum, look for a guarantee that you can renew the policy (it would be pointless to buy a policy that won't let you renew because you're sick), coverage for all care levels (skilled, intermediate and home care), coverage that can't be cancelled due to advancing age, that has no limitation on prior hospitalization, that covers Alzheimer's, and home health care coverage with no prior stay required in a nursing home or hospital (some illnesses are progressive, not acute).

Run from high-pressure sales tactics when buying insurance. Deal only with reputable agents and insurance companies rated A or better by Best's Reports, an independent rating firm.

Medicaid Planning
This offshoot of estate planning is even more important for people remarrying than it is for long-term marrieds (who have joint children, parallel interests and concerns, and a long history of devotion to one another).

Medicaid is a joint federal/state program that provides medical assistance for people who are destitute. The goal of Medicaid planning to keep one person solvent if the other requires expensive medical attention, such as nursing home care. It would seem to be a fair division in upper-middle-class homes if, in the event one spouse had to go into a nursing home, the couple would be required to split their assets, with half being used for the ailing person and the other half reserved for the at-home spouse, who may or may not be healthy. This division wouldn't be fair if the couple had very little money, however, because then the at-home spouse wouldn't have enough to live on.

But the government has its own rules. Only a limited amount of skilled nursing care is paid for under Medicare at this moment. You are responsible for the rest, unless you become eligible for Medicaid, which means you must have only limited assets.

Suppose one of you has to go into a nursing home for an extended period. To understand how that affects the other's finances, you have to know what you can keep and still have your spouse qualify for Medicaid. You can keep certain exempt assets, like the family home, a car and some personal possessions, such as jewelry and furs. You can keep a limited monthly income from pensions, Social Security or investments. That income is meager and varies from state to state. You can keep a small portion of whatever remaining nonexempt assets you as a couple have amassed (either individually or jointly) including cash, securities, a vacation home, other investments. This figure also varies state to state.

If the person who's sick transfers all of his or her assets to the other spouse in an effort to preserve some capital, he or she can qualify immediately for Medicaid to pay nursing home bills. The at-home spouse can refuse to pay any of the nursing home costs, arguing that he or she needs all the money to live. But keep in mind that you're in a battle with the government, which can take its emotional and financial toll. Remember, too, that the state has a right to seek contributions from the at-home spouse. And while the at-home spouse will not be uprooted from the family home, the government can slap a lien on the house equal to the nursing home expenses, which will be satisfied when the house is sold or the at-home spouse dies.

(Revised Medicare provisions are being discussed by our elected officials now, so watch for meaningful changes in the Medicare and Medicaid rules.)

Power of Attorney

A final word about the unpredictability of health. The line between good and poor health is often fuzzy—as in the case of someone who is lucid some or the time and disoriented at other times. It also can be jumped at a moment's notice, such as when a healthy person is brain-damaged as a result of an auto accident. That's why it's important to have a simple legal document called a durable power of attorney. It gives another person legal authority to act for you. A durable power of attorney can be set up so that it goes into effect only if you become incapacitated. Called a "springing" durable power of attorney, it's the one many people opt for because they want control over decisions when they're healthy, but need a trusted decision-maker when they're incapacitated. (Make sure you and the person you designate to act for you are clear about the definition of incapacitation.)

It's typical for spouses to appoint one another as the attorney-in-fact, or for a parent to appoint one or more trusted children. In a remarriage, the choice of attorney-in-fact may be a delicate issue because of the inherent distrust children feel toward the new spouse. Only the person creating the durable power of attorney knows (or senses) who has the best judgment and would act in his or her best interest.

WHERE TO LIVE

As people get older, they often want to simplify their lives, not make their day-to-day existence more complicated. They contemplate selling homes and moving into condominiums or rental apartments, where others will assume the maintenance.

After you've assessed your needs and wants, remarriage at this time in your life gives you a natural opportunity to change your living arrangements. As a couple, you have to determine your overall financial position. If you have little capital or sources for future income, selling both your homes, renting an apartment, and investing the accumulated equity may make sense. Too, you have to think about your lifestyle. If you plan to travel extensively, consider renting or buying a condo. Then mowing the lawn and cleaning the pool become the building management's responsibility, not yours. If, however, you're passionate about gardening and carpentry, you might want to have a place of your own to work on.

Protecting Your Spouse's Right to Live in Your House

A home is often the single greatest asset of any couple. Frequently in a remarriage when the couple buys a house together, each spouse wants to ensure that his or her share of this property goes, eventually, to children of a former marriage. Even still, neither spouse wants to see the surviving spouse squeezed out of the house simply because the heirs want or need the money and try to force a sale. One estate planning tool frequently used to forestall that possibility is to have each spouse create a marital life estate trust which allows the surviving spouse full use of the house until his or her death. Then half the house goes to the wife's children and half to the husband's. (More about estate planning in the next chapter.)

YOUR SOCIAL SECURITY BENEFITS

Social Security regulations are so wordy and complex that it's no wonder people are confused about what remarriage will do to benefits.

Many a widow who has been receiving survivor's benefits from Social Security since her husband's death fears that remarriage will threaten that regular check. It won't. When you remarry you are still entitled to collect these survivor's benefits—no matter how much money you new spouse has. That's still true even if you were divorced from your now-deceased former spouse, as long as you're over 60 and not entitled to a higher benefit based on your own earnings.

Some people are concerned that remarriage will mean that as a couple you will receive less Social Security than you would if you lived together as an unmarried couple. But that's not the case. When you're eligible for Social Security, you and your spouse will independently receive benefits based on how long each of you worked, and how much you paid into the system. When you're married, you have the option of receiving benefits based on what you paid into the system, or one-half of your spouse's benefits, whichever is greater.

If you remarry, don't expect to share in a former spouse's retirement benefits. But you can collect Social Security retirement benefits based on your new spouse's earnings record as long as you're over 62 and take care of your spouse's under-16-year-old (or over 16 and disabled) child. The marriage must have lasted at least one year when the wife or husband applied for benefits—or the couple must have had a child.

If your new spouse dies, you are eligible for Social Security benefits if you're over 60 (or over 50 and disabled) and meet certain requirements. The marriage must have lasted at least nine months before your spouse's death, or a shorter marriage has to have ended by accidental death, or you must have had a child together. (These requirements are designed to discourage scheming people from entering into a marriage simply to collect benefits.)

A widow who remarries, but is single again due to divorce, annulment or the death of a second husband, can reapply for her first husband's veteran benefits, assuming he was in the military.

WHAT THE CHILDREN WILL SAY

Kids will be kids—even when they're adults. Adult children's objections to the marriage will be expressed differently and will be over different issues, but rest assured that there will always be one adult child who begins a conversation about your remarriage with the phrase, "I know it's none of my business, but...."

Like kids, adult children resist change. It's not that their daily existence will be threatened by the introduction of a new person. It probably won't. They might be genuinely happy about the marriage. Or they simply might be relieved that they are no longer primarily responsible for the parent's emotional or financial well-being.

"It has nothing to do with whether or not I like Sam," Philip says. "I like the fact that I don't have to worry about my mother daily. Sam does. I've stopped giving her the extra $300 a month that I initiated when Dad died. And quite selfishly, now my wife and I can go on vacation and not feel obligated to ask my mother to come along."

More often, however, adult children are leery or angry. Sometimes long-buried feelings of conflicting loyalties arise. In case of divorce, it can be most evident when the adult child realizes he or she actually likes the new stepparent. When the widowed parent remarries, the child might feel guilty about treating the stepparent as a parent. Or incensed. "I see my father giving things to his new wife that he never gave to my mother. And she worked infinitely harder than this woman."

If all this isn't complicated enough, there are additional issues addling adult children. Some of them deal with logistics, some with behavior; most deal with finances.

Logistically, the new relationship throws "who's going to be where when" into chaos.

"I've always looked forward to celebrating Passover at my mother's house," Anne said. "But that's going to change as soon as she marries Murray. They're going to move to Florida [near one of his sons] and it's too expensive to fly my whole family down there each year. Besides, it wouldn't be the same."

Behaviorally, change evokes worry. Adult children don't know how they're going to establish an adult-to-adult relationship with this new person. What are they going to call him or her? They don't know what is expected from them if this person gets sick or needs their help in any way. They don't know how this new relationship will change their parent—and in turn how it will affect their parent-adult child relationship.

"My mother was always available for babysitting, baking, and helping me when a problem arose and I couldn't be home," explains Sharon, a 43-year-old divorced saleswoman. "Now she's out at the gym four mornings a week and will be taking a month-long cruise with her new husband. It blows my mind. She's become a hip woman at 78. That's not how I envisioned these years."

Sharon admits the remarriage has forced her to reflect on what she expects from her mother. "She's no longer on call—which I guess is what I wanted from her. Too, I'm envious. She has renewed vitality and the time, money, and mate to do pretty much what she wants."

Change also can push an adult child to reassess his or her own marriage.

"I know it sounds crazy," Bea says, "but I was so frightened of change that I figured I'd just have to live with my husband until he died, just as my mother had lived with my father until his death. My mother's choice to remarry gave

me the courage I needed to make a change. Instead of sitting at home waiting for my former husband to be killed in an accident—and feeling guilty for having those thoughts—I decided to take matters into my own hands. I divorced him. Although I haven't remarried yet, I now believe I have a chance to meet someone who is kind and caring—just like Mom did."

Adult children often like the parent's new partner. Sometimes they know the person well because he or she is a long-time family friend. Sometimes they're happy because the person is kind to the parent. They become suspicious, however, when they think this new mate will take advantage of their parent.

All eyes rivet on the woman who marries a younger man or a man who marries a younger woman, for example. "Adult children see this as exploitive—whether or not it is," says Dr. Florence Kaslow, director of the Florida Couples and Family Institute in West Palm Beach. "In the case of the older woman, people ask 'Why would he want to marry someone older unless it's for her money?' and in the case of the older man, it's 'She's only after his money.'" When a person marries someone closer in age and in net worth, there's not as much distrust."

A New York City attorney tells of a visit from the 45-year-old son of a 78-year-old widower who was planning to marry a woman eighteen years his junior. "This woman is coarse and crude—a real sharpie," the son confided to the attorney. "A gold digger. I've asked Dad to call you to discuss a prenuptial."

The 78-year-old came in to talk about a prenuptial agreement. He wanted to put about a third of his estate into a trust that his new wife could draw on for as long as she lived. The rest of his estate would go to his son.

When the attorney mentioned the son's objections to the marriage, the father replied. "I never had it so good. She's fun, exciting, and makes me feel twenty years younger. I know it will cost me, but what better way to spend my money? Far better than on medicine and a nursing home."

WHAT YOU OWE THE CHILDREN

Issues of finance and inheritance seem to sir up the most concern when people remarry at a later age. How will the marriage affect the support an adult child is getting? (One in three young adults in their twenties receives some financial help from parents.) What will the remarriage mean to inheritance? What will become of family heirlooms or ordinary objects that have sentimental value? Will the adult child continue to provide some financial support to a parent who's remarrying?

"It's a complicated question of accountability when you're contemplating a remarriage and have adult children," says Boston attorney Mark Levinson. "It's as if you have these children looking over your shoulder and you have to seek their permission to marry—obliquely or directly." Certainly, in the case of remarriage, more parents will solicit the opinions of their adult children than they would the opinions of young children. And they listen more carefully to any objections raised.

Talking About Your Finances

People in their fifties, sixties, seventies and beyond often consider financial information private and balk at the thought of sharing inheritance matters with their children. In a simple family situation where two parents split their estate between two children who feel equally loved and are in the same socioeconomic bracket, perhaps nothing need be said. The will would speak for itself. But remarriage means you're bringing another person, often a complete stranger, into the family picture. Understand that whatever you think of this new union, the children don't think it's as important as the one in which they were conceived. And in the case of inheritance, adult children expect money or property to follow a bloodline, not a wedding band. They will probably refer to the new spouse as "my mother's husband" or "my father's wife" rather than "my stepfather" or "my stepmother"—further drawing the psychological distinction between blood and marriage. Whether it's conscious or not, everyone realizes that the relationship between the "steps" will take longer to develop than when children are younger, mainly because there's less time together.

Assuming you have a good relationship with your adult children, you owe them time to talk over their concerns and expectations—and yours.

You're not alone if you have to clear your throat and take a deep breath before you discuss the dollars and cents of inheritance. It's a subject that evokes powerful emotions—even in first marriages. It raises several uncomfortable issues that are difficult to maneuver around: death, money, and how parents perceive their children. Throw a new spouse into the mix and the province already rife with symbolism and ambiguity becomes even more so.

Yet the goal is to avoid the mistrust that comes with not knowing.

For anyone to urge universal disclosure of estate or inheritance plans to children would be imprudent. We have different relationships with each child. They, too, are different from one another. We have to know our own children. They are, after all, still people, people who fall all over the spectrum between caring and crass, selfless and selfish, generous and greedy. A grasping daughter will probably become more grasping when she hears about the remarriage. An adaptable son will be more amenable to the idea. "Jonathon and Liza are terrific people and I'd tell them everything about my finances," Rochelle said. "But Lila, she's different. I haven't spoken to her for five years and she's done terrible things to her siblings and me. I don't feel I owe her anything, not even talk."

Children with whom you have a good relationship deserve to know where they stand, emotionally and financially, as a result of this marriage. If the family relationship has been fairly harmonious, you'll be surprised how effective the trust you've built up will be in relieving the anxiety surrounding the topic.

You're Still in Charge

Acknowledging your children's involvement in this marriage by soliciting their opinions does not mean you give them decision-making authority over your life—no matter how much respect you have for them. And it's inappropriate for them to demand it. "Sometimes I'm appalled by adults who treat their parents as children, threatening not to have anything to do with the parent if he or she remarries," says one Atlanta attorney. "These kids never treated their parents well to begin with and are only concerned they'll be nosed out of an inheritance. I want to jump across the table and scream to these parents that they don't have to listen to their kids or allow themselves to be bullied."

After they're widowed, people are concerned about protecting their assets for children. But that their choice, not the kids'. There's nothing written anywhere that says you have to leave your children a hefty inheritance.

"I've always told my children I'd give them their college education and $10,000 for a down payment on a house," says Larsen, a real estate broker in Minneapolis. "That's what I felt I owed them. Nothing more. Yet," he continues, "that doesn't mean I don't want them to inherit anything. When I married for the third time I told them we had worked out an agreement which says anything I earned before our marriage goes to my children, anything Gretchen earned [as a doctor] before our marriages goes to her children. Anything we earn from now on goes to each other—to do with what we want."

Most people do feel an emotional bonding with their children—strong enough that they'd like to leave them some inheritance and no financial indebtedness.

ALLAYING CHILDREN'S INHERITANCE JITTERS

Naturally, even before you discuss the inheritance with your children, you should discuss it with your intended or new spouse, who should be aware of your financial loyalties, concerns and obligations. You may have told your daughter she'll be inheriting your art collection. You may have promised your granddaughter that you'll give her the money she'll need to buy into a dental practice. You and your siblings may send your elderly mother additional support payments each month. Or as part of a separation agreement with a former spouse, you may have an insurance policy naming him or her the beneficiary. Make it clear to your partner that you have an ethical commitment to uphold these financial promises and that that commitment is not in conflict with the love you have for him or her.

Prenuptial agreements are recommended for remarried with substantial assets simply because you've spent a great deal of time building those assets (usually with a former spouse) and, should they evaporate, there is less time to rebuild them.

Once the two of you have a fair understanding of how you plan to allocate assets now and after you die, you might want to call a family gathering (one family at a time, please).

If you've drawn up a prenuptial, paint a broad picture of the thinking behind it and how it will affect your adult children.

If you're in the process of drawing up wills (universally recommended when you remarry), tell your children what you hope to accomplish. (Many attorneys now videotape their clients when they sign new wills and ask them questions to verify that they are in sound mind and not being coerced into signing. Then, if adult children question the will later, they can see how much in control the parent was.) Adult children should know the rationale behind your decisions, especially if they are not the immediate beneficiaries of you estate, you have done something unusual with your property, or the estate is not divided equally among the children.

If, for example, you have created a marital life estate trust, which ensures that your property will eventually go to the children, tell them why you've done this. "While we've bought our house as tenants in common, which means my share can be left to you immediately, I want to make certain that Millie is able to live in the home for as long as she wants, should I die first. She wants the same for me. What we've done is set up a trust that allows that. When we're both gone, my half will go my children, her half to hers." (Many different types of control can be imposed on these trusts. The trustee can be someone other than the surviving spouse. The trustee might be required to make periodic reports to the final beneficiaries, the adult children. The spouse can be prohibited from selling any property in the marital life estate trust.)

Or suppose you've lent your stepdaughter $25,000 for a down payment on a home, but you intend to forgive the loan if it's not repaid at the time of your death. You might tell your children so that they can understand your motives. "If Nicole can't repay the loan, my will is going to forgive her. I wanted her to have the house and she has not been able to build up the financial reservoir that you have. I know you'll understand that this gift doesn't affect my deep love for you."

GIFTS: NOW MAY BE A BETTER TIME THAN LATER

Talking about inheritance presents a wonderful opportunity for adult children to be asked what objects have symbolic value to them and what objects of yours they would like to have—either now, or when the parent dies. Such a meeting among one family resulted in one of the sons hauling away to his own home the piano he fondly remembered his mother playing, and a daughter leaving with portrait of her parents that she had always loved. The new wife was secretly delighted. "We had no room for piano, and I really didn't care to have the painting around," she confided.

Gift giving while we're well and able to experience the joy of the recipient can be great fun. It can also be very reassuring to adult children whose parents are remarrying. If they were conditioned to equate money and love, they feel bolstered by the gift. If they are in need of it, they don't feel that the new relationship will mean financial abandonment.

People who can afford it can give up to $10,000 annually to as many people as they want without having to pay a gift tax, and, as a couple, you can give $20,000. If gifts are made each year, this annual exclusion can achieve substantial estate tax savings for heirs of large estates.

If you don't want to give money, consider making a gift of life insurance to a child. The policy is on your own life. To keep it out of your estate (and therefore not subject to federal estate tax), the policy must be given at least three years before your death. The value of the policy at the time of the gift is subject to gift tax, but that's far less than the amount the policy will pay at the time of your death. If you own the policy, the proceeds are included in your taxable estate. If your child owns it (which means he or she has to pay premiums—though, of course, you could gift him the money for the payments), they are not.

Aside from the $10,000/$20,000 annual exemption, there are other transfers of money or property that are exempt from gift tax. Of special interest to remarrieds are gifts between spouses, payment of medical bills (of relatives or friends), and of school tuition (to assist grandchildren, for example).

PARENTING ISSUES REVISITED

When you remarry later in life, you don't expect daily parenting issues to become a factor in the relationship. But, more and more, as adult children divorce or find themselves in financial straits because they're unable to get or hold down a job, they turn to the parents for real (as well as emotional) shelter and money. Lo and behold, the remarried couple has to come to terms with a new philosophical dilemma: What's a parent's financial responsibility to adult children?

Chantel and Robert are just such a couple. Chantel had been divorced for many years and Robert a few when they married in Cleveland. He was 54 and a teacher at the time; she was 47 and a human resources manager at a bank. Their earnings were about equal. She had some equity in a home she owned; he had little, having given up most of his material possessions as a result of two previous divorces. None of their children lived at home anymore.

Five years after their marriage, Robert was offered an early retirement package, which he took. Chantel continued to work, advancing her level of responsibility and income, until two years ago. That's when they decided to retire to a small town in Connecticut near the Long Island Sound. They had just settled in when Chantel's only child, Keith, who had been working in the aerospace industry in Los Angeles, lost his job.

Robert: "I have to give him credit for trying to find a job. He had taken his wife and child to Denver to look for work, but it wasn't any better there. That's when he called and asked if they could come live with us while they got their act together."

Chantel: "It was hard. Initially, none of us was working, so even though the house is large, we were still together all the time. And Keith's marriage was falling apart. His wife is an alcoholic...and a mean drunk. Eventually she moved out and there was an ugly custody battle, for which Keith's father and I split legal expenses."

Robert: "The situation now is that Chantel has gone back to work as a full-time consultant in the human resources field, because our expenses for Keith and the baby are so high that our present income can't cover them. If Chantel were happy about this, I might not say a word. But she's complaining about commuting into Manhattan—and frankly, I don't think she should have to do it. This is Keith's responsibility. He's working at some menial job. He's an adult and should be footing the bills for his son and himself. I'm not against helping adult children when they need it. My youngest lived with us after graduation. But I told him at that time that he was out of here after three months, and, interestingly, within that three months he found a job and left."

Even if this were a first marriage for both Robert and Chantel, this would be a difficult situation. Because they haven't had a history of parenting together, it's even more difficult. They don't know how to react to each other's styles. They need to talk about:

- Why Chantel feels it's her responsibility to support Keith.
- How to take Robert's reaction into consideration.
- What the best way is to speed Keith into independent living. (They might agree to pay for additional training that would help him get a more lucrative job. They might set a time limit on his stay. They might give Keith enough money for a security deposit on an apartment and have him move. If they don't mind Keith and the baby living with them as long as they're reimbursed, they might ask for rent and household expense money.)

If the couple is too emotional about the problem, they will need professional help—a certified family or couple's counselor—to facilitate conversation and help them work toward a mutually agreeable solution so they can present a unified front to Keith.

AT LAST, ANOTHER CHOICE

"Here's a dilemma we never thought about when we first married," Herman said. "Where are we going to be buried?" Herman and Flo, both 71, are not alone. They laugh about this new wrinkle in their six-year-old marriage, but theirs is a frequent dilemma among those who remarry later in life.

Most remarriages after sixty involve at least one widow or widower. Their first marriages might have been very happy. At the time of the first spouse's death, the surviving spouse probably had every intention of being buried near or next to his or her spouse someday.

When the widow remarries and spends many happy years with a new spouse, the "plot plot" thickens.

Children of a first marriage might express strong feelings about wanting their parents to be buried together. "And that's understandable," says Flo, who's more concerned about the dilemma than Herman. "I feel it's important to consider their wishes."

But there's another side. Herman, who was a bachelor before marrying Flo, could be buried in a family plot, but would prefer to buy a plot for Flo and himself. She's not sure she wants that. She's vacillating between being buried near her first husband and being buried near Herman. They have not come to any decisions, yet. "Believe it or not, I'm thinking of cremation," says Flo. "I may have half my ashes buried with my first husband and half buried with Herman."

All of this points out, once again, that even up to the very end, remarrieds must come up with creative solutions to peculiar problems.

Chapter Ten

Estate Planning:
Assets, Heirlooms—and What About the Kids?

By the time people reach remarrying age, they usually don't ask the question: Why worry about estate planning if I don't have an 'estate'?" They know the answer.

"I'm not sure if we have 'assets' or 'stuff,' but we do have kids and we have to make certain that everyone and everything is accounted for— eventually," says Kathie, a Miami physician remarried for eight years.

Nor by this time are people any longer likely to be comforted by the notion that they're too young to die. They usually know of at least one contemporary who has died—either in an accident or from an untimely illness.

Yet people still stall when it comes to estate planning.

Merely recognizing a need for estate planning doesn't propel a couple into action. In a candid admission to a group of remarried couples some years ago, a Los Angeles matrimonial lawyer whose specialty is stepfamilies said, "I counsel clients on the need for an estate plan. I lecture on its importance. Yet I, myself, have not adequately redesigned my estate plan to take into account my present stepfamily arrangement. I can't face up to it, even though my husband urges me to do so. As soon as I think about redrafting my will, I come face to face with the many difficult loyalty issues that exist in our family. Who will take care of my children? Who will get my money? Who will live in my house?"

Even if you haven't met with an estate planner (who can be a lawyer, a trained financial planner, a Certified Life Underwriter (CLU), or an accountant specially trained in this field), you probably have done some estate planning. You have named a beneficiary on your insurance policy. The house deed lists you as owner. The safe-deposit box at the bank is in joint name. You own the car you drive; your spouse owns the other. Perhaps a separation agreement you signed requires you to leave some portion of your estate to your children from a prior marriage. Perhaps your spouse has a bank account in trust for a child.

Whether planned or patched together, you have an estate plan.

For remarrieds, reconstruction isn't easy. Splintered loyalties, new responsibilities and changed needs force remarried couples to create estate plans that are the paper equivalents of Rube Goldberg's mechanical contrivances. Plans must take into consideration the makeup of this new, complicated family, the assets of spouses, their goals, and the best way to put the pieces together so that the aims are accomplished. And they must ensure that each spouse has complete control over how his or her property is distributed after death—as complete as the law and prior agreements allow.

WHO'S KIN?

A remarried family can get complicated. There are relatives, step-relatives, and quasi-kin (a former mother-in-law, for example). There is often confusion as to the family's boundaries. For example, are children who "visit" considered part of the new family, and are they to be treated the same as custodial children?

Before scheduling a meeting with an estate planner, draw up a list of family members for whom you have financial responsibility, both legally and morally. It gives you an idea of the scope of the family, and provides the estate planner with a scorecard of who's who in your family. It will also save you some money because the estate planner doesn't have to spend hours deciphering who the players are.

BOX—PUT ON ONE PAGE

"ABOUT THE FAMILY" WORKSHEET

For your convenience, prepare a separate worksheet for each of you.

Your Personal Information

Name_____

Address_____

Phone_____ Fax_____ Email_____

Any other names you've had_____

Occupation_____

Business address_____

Business Phone_____Business Fax_____

Business Email_____

Social Security number_____

Date and place of birth_____

This marriage: date and place _____

Names and addresses of former spouses_____
_____

Dates and reasons for former marriages ending (death or divorce)_____
_____

Children from Prior Marriages

	First	Second	Third
Name	————	————	————
Date of birth	————	————	————
Place of birth	————	————	————
Address	————	————	————
Social Security number	————	————	————
Explanation of present support arrangements (if still dependent)			
If independent and applicable			
Name	————	————	————
Name of his or her spouse	————	————	————
Names of children (your grandchildren)	————	————	————

Children from This Marriage

	First	Second	Third
Name	————	————	————
Date of birth	————	————	————
Place of birth	————	————	————
Social Security number	————	————	————

Other Dependents

	First	Second	Third
Name	————	————	————
Address	————	————	————
Relationship	————	————	————
Age	————	————	————
Present support arrangements	————	————	————

END BOX

WHO OWNS WHAT?

You can't give away what you don't own. So before making estate plans, inventory your major possessions. Key in this exercise is knowing what the different forms of ownership mean. (Many states have slight variations of wording, so check with your lawyer if you have a question.) A brief overview:

Joint Tenacy
Each joint tenant owns an equal share of the property with all other joint tenants. The share of the first tenant to die must go to the remaining joint tenants, even if there's a will to the contrary.

Community Property
In the eight community property states (Arizona, California, Idaho, Nevada, New Mexico, Texas, Washington and Wisconsin), any property a spouse earns or acquires during a marriage becomes the property of the marriage (with a few exceptions), which means each of you, owns half the property. Each of you can leave your one-half share of community property to whomever you want; the other half belongs to your spouse. You have no right to give that away.

Separate Property
This is defined differently depending on whether you live in a community property state or in a common law property state. In community property states, all property that isn't community property is held separately. In common law property states, separate property means all property each spouse owns individually—unless there's a written contract to the contrary.

Tenancy in Common
In this shared ownership, you can leave your portion of the property held as tenants in common to whomever you choose, unless restricted by a contract. Unlike joint tenancy, with tenancy in common the owners' shares to not have to be equal.

Partnership
Property that is owned by business partners. Most partnerships have an agreement stating how a partner's financial interests will be handled in the event of death.

Corporate Shares
The bylaws of a corporation or shareholders' agreement generally dictate how the shares in a closely held or small corporation are handled in case of a shareholder's death.

With this information in hand, draw up a list of what you own and how it's owned. Include in that list:

Assets
- Checking accounts
- Savings accounts
- Money market funds/accounts
- Certificates of deposit (CDs)
- Mutual funds
- Government bonds
- Stocks
- Bonds
- Precious metals
- Automobiles (and any other vehicles, such as boats, planes)

- Art, antiques, or valuable furniture
- Jewelry, furs
- Money owed to you
- Shares of limited partnerships
- Profit-sharing plans and stock options
- Vested interests in retirement plans, such as IRAs or Keoghs
- Annuities
- Cash value in life insurance policies
- Other personal property of value

Real Estate
- Your home (less the mortgage)
- Second home (less the mortgage)
- Investment property (less the mortgage)

Business Property
- Business ownership
- Miscellaneous receivables
- Royalties, trademarks, patents, copyrights

Liabilities
- Type and amount of debt owed
- Credit card debt
- Bank loans (excluding the mortgages)
- Personal debt (judgments and accrued child support)
- Taxes (back taxes owed plus this year's liability)
- Other

When you're all finished subtract your liabilities from all your assets to determine your net worth. Understand that this is just an estimate. Net worths fluctuate daily.

THE PERSONAL DECISIONS

What do you hope to accomplish when you leave money or property to heirs?

People in second, third and fourth marriages usually have multiple goals because the picture of family responsibilities fits into the 11X17 variety, not the 5X7 size. Setting up a system that will carry out your goals is the heart of an estate plan. Once you've clarified yours, dividing the dollars is simply a technical matter that can be done by attorneys—at a minimum cost or at great expense, depending on the complexity of the goals and the size of the estate.

Prime your own thinking by reviewing the following list of goals. Add what's important to you and then prioritize the list. Again, you and your spouse may want to prepare separate lists so each of you can develop your own goals.

Goal setting is different from goal implementation. As you implement your plans, you'll want to take into consideration estate and income taxes, attorney fees, the speed of the distribution process to your heirs, and ways to avoid conflict over your decisions. Strategies for those will be discussed later.

ESTATE GOALS WORKSHEET FOR _____

Name

I want to...

_____ provide security for my surviving spouse.

_____ be certain my children have a guardian of my choosing.

_____ provide money to be used for children's education.

_____ keep the business in the family.

_____ assure the continuity of the business.

_____ make certain my assets eventually wind up with my children from a former marriage.

_____ provide our child with financial benefits similar to those my older children had.

_____ treat heirs equitably (not necessarily equally).

_____ provide for the special needs of a particular heir.

_____ provide support for my elderly parent(s).

_____ designate certain items (from heirlooms to "stuff") for certain heirs.

_____ eliminate certain potential heirs from receiving any property from me.

_____ protect my property from medical/nursing home costs.

_____ leave a portion of my estate to a charity.

_____ Other (list)

ESTATE PLANNING

If we played a word association game and someone said "estate planning," 50 percent of us would probably say "death" and the other half would probably say "wills"

Those who said "death" would always be right.

Those who said "wills," however, would be substituting just one segment of the total estate-planning picture for the entirety. In fact, wills aren't necessary to pass along assets. You can transfer property and assets to others without wills by giving gifts when you're alive, owning something jointly so that the property will go to the co-owner when you die, or naming someone as the beneficiary on a life insurance policy or pension fund. You might have a partnership, separation or prenuptial agreement dictating the way property you own is to be disbursed. You may have established a trust (a legal entity) that transfers property to a beneficiary at the time of your death. Or you may have a bank account that acts as a trust.

In short, estate planning isn't just wills.

BUT WILLS ARE STILL IMPORTANT

So why all the pressure to draw up a will? Why do lawyers look askance at people who don't have them? Why does Dick Dunn, a retired cleric who headed the stepfamily ministry at the Roswell Methodist Church in Georgia, insist that before he counseled people considering a remarriage, they begin drawing up a will? "The complications of one or both spouses in a subsequent marriage dying without a will are too great," says Reverend Dunn.

What can cause the complications?

Children

Dependent children are the primary reason to have a will. As a parent, you want to have a say in who's going to rear them and look after the property you're leaving to them. You're dealing with your most valuable asset. An arbitrary state law shouldn't make decisions of such major importance.

Everything You Haven't Accounted for Elsewhere

Suppose you have things of value—sentimental or real—that you want to give to certain people or organizations. Or you won the lottery and came into an unexpected inheritance and died before you had time to give it away or put it in a trust. Without a will, state law dictates how that property would be distributed.

State laws differ. If you die without a will, your spouse and your children usually are the beneficiaries—though the percentages of what each gets varies state by state. And children are all treated equally—whether they are children of a first marriage or children of a remarriage. That makes it especially difficult on young, dependent children who need greater financial support than adult children do. If you have no children, some of your property might go to your parents.

If you want to know exactly how your state handles intestacy (dying without a will), leaf through your state's legal code, which is available at a public or law library, or speak to an attorney.

For remarrieds, things can get messy if an old will is in effect when you die. While states won't allow your present spouse to be disinherited (in effect, revoking the claims of a former spouse), any specific gifts made to your former spouse under an old will might still go to him or her. If, for example, you specifically named your former wife as the beneficiary of farmland that has been in your family for centuries in a will you made many years ago and you never destroyed or revoked the will, she might become "mistress of the meadows"—even if that's the last thing you'd want.

Even when you've carefully plotted out who gets what, time has a way of altering those Solomon-like judgments.

"I inherited a slew of antiques," Jack explains. "I wanted them to stay in the family, so in my will I left them to my children—since Cassy and I have no children together. We've been married about fourteen years now and my kids have told me they hate antiques. So I'm changing my will again. Cassy will get

all of them. She can do whatever she wants with the pieces. If she remarries and her new husband winds up with them, that's fine with me. Anyway, how will I know?"

WHO'S GOING TO CARE FOR CHILDREN?

This is often the toughest question you'll face when preparing a will.

Under normal circumstances, when one parent dies the other biological parent assumes custody of their joint children—even after a divorce. But remarriage often challenges this assumption. In all probability, for instance, a ten-year-old child who has been living with her mother, stepfather and half-sister for six years would be shipped off to live with her biological father after her mother's death. That's assuming he wants her and is capable of caring for her. Capable means competent; it doesn't mean that parent is the better of the two men (father and stepfather) to do the job of child rearing. And it doesn't take into consideration the needs of the child, who might be much better off in the bosom of a caring and familiar stepfather and half-sister during this traumatic time.

"I cringe to think Elliot might someday have custody of the children," says Diane of her former husband. "To me he's a religious lunatic, cheap beyond belief, mean, dishonest and unstable. It's especially repugnant because the children really love Gene and feel as if he's their real dad. But my separation agreement has me locked into naming Elliot as guardian. If nothing else, that's reason enough to keep me alive and healthy until the children are adults," Diane jokes halfheartedly.

Wills generally should not violate anything you've already agreed to in a separation or prenuptial agreement. In Diane's case, however, she might try naming Gene as the children's guardian in her will and hope Elliot won't contest the custody choice in court if she dies while the children are still minors. If he does, her case for violating the separation agreement would be strengthened if in the will or in a note attached to the will she explains her reasoning. The reasons would have to be more than a personal vendetta if she wanted the court to overturn the separation agreement. Powerful arguments would be that the absent parent hadn't provided support, hadn't seen the child for years, had a history of alcohol or drug abuse, or was mentally unstable or physically abusive. Even if a father were any of those things, however, there is no guarantee the court would decide against his guardianship in a contested battle. A stepparent still has no legal standing with regard to stepchildren. But in current custody decisions, more and more judges consider the length of the remarriage, how involved the biological father has remained in the children's lives, what the children want, and what is perceived to be in the best interests of the children.

The process of naming guardians for custodial children in a remarriage is similar to the way it's done in a first marriage.

- You name someone you trust to rear your children in a manner you'd approve.
- You make certain you choose someone who is willing, ready and able to do the job. Discuss it with him or her first.
- You name an alternate guardian, in case at the time of your death the primary guardian can't assume the responsibility, or in the event you and primary guardian die at the same time.

Who's going to manage the property (money and investments) you leave to a minor child?

In most cases, the person to whom you have entrusted the child's physical and emotional care is the person you'd want to control the child's money—even if that person is a former spouse. That's because you assume the property would be used honestly to provide for the child's normal living expenses and health and education needs.

But—and this is a big "but"—what if one of the reasons you and your former spouse divorced was because you couldn't tolerate each other's handling of or attitudes about money? In that case, you'd probably want to name another person to act as your child's property manager. That person may or may not be your present spouse, depending on whether the web of emotions surrounding the remarriage is entangled with bitterness and revenge. It would also depend on whether your present spouse could or would want to have a continuing relationship—albeit a financial one—with your former spouse.

Prior Orders
Sometimes there's something in a will that contradicts an earlier agreement. Often the agreement was signed so long ago, people forget about it or don't think it's still in force. Sometimes people deliberately try to slip something into a will that counters an agreement because the agreement in onerous to them. Unless the prior agreement is deemed illegal or no longer valid, it prevails and takes precedence over the will.

WHAT TO TAKE TO THE LAWYER'S OFFICE

You can draw up your own will. Yet even in the simplest "no children-no assets" remarriage, it's safest to seek the counsel of an estate attorney.

Choose an attorney with whom you feel comfortable, because, as Atlanta estate attorney Ann Salo says, "Though I deal in a very narrow band of a person's life, I share intimate details about family and finances. The shingle I really need is the one that reads 'estate therapist'."

Stuff the following into your briefcase after you've chosen your estate therapist and are ready to draw up a will:

- A list of who owns what, how it's owned, and its approximate value.
- The "About the Family" worksheet
- The "What My Estate Goals Are" worksheet
- Copies of previous wills, if any
- Insurance policies
- Divorce or separation decrees, if any
- Your prenuptial agreement, if you have one
- Tax returns for the past three years
- Deferred compensation contracts, pension or profit-sharing agreements

Before signing a will, reexamine your estate goals worksheet to be certain that your primary goals are reflected.

THE PROBATE PANIC

Why do people shudder when probate is mentioned? Though it sounds like an ominous procedure, it's simply a legal process by which a court approves your will and formally appoints the executor you've named, who then oversees the distribution of your property. The proceedings are generally mere formalities unless the will is contested or, if you died intestate (without a will) because it hard to locate the people who might have an interest in the estate.

What causes the initial shudder is that most people have heard horror stories about how long the process takes. It needn't take more than a few months, but it can take years if there are snags. People are also concerned about the cost of probate. The larger the estate the executor has to administer, the larger the commission he or she receives from that estate (although if the executor is also a beneficiary, that can be a plus—tax-wise.) Lawyers generally charge on an hourly basis, rather than take a percentage of the estate.

There are a number of estate planning vehicles that move assets out of the probate loop—life insurance, gifts, trusts, joint ownership, bank accounts—all of which will be discussed. One thing to keep in mind: Avoiding probate doesn't mean your estate avoids estate tax. If tax is applicable, it has to be paid, whether your assets are probated or not.

TALK ABOUT TRUSTS

"It's curious that the word 'trust' when it's used in connection with estate planning connotes a lack of trust," writes John Levy, executive director of the Jung Institute in San Francisco and an expert in the psychology of inheritance. But it shouldn't. Certainly not among husbands and wives in remarriages. Trusts can be helpful in managing and protecting property for the person you want to benefit. Some trusts can be set up within the framework of your will; others operate outside of it. And some sidestep probate.

Let's look at some trust that can solve problems for remarrieds.

The Living Trust
To those of us who think of a trust as an instrument that springs to life after death, this oxymoron is as appealing as a ghoul is. So I prefer to speak of a living trust by its more palatable name, a revocable trust. While you live, you effectively own all the property you transfer to your revocable trust and can do with it what you want—keep it, sell it, spend it or give it

away. When you die, the trust becomes operational and all the property passes to the people or organizations named in it.

For some, living trusts are unnecessary. A young couple with relatively few assets probably just needs life insurance and a will, which is less costly to draft than a trust.

But other people should consider living trusts: those with very large estates who want to avoid probate, those who want their assets distributed promptly when they die, or those who want to make the distribution of their assets more difficult to contest.

The Q-Tip Trust

This formidable estate planning tool, the qualified terminable interest property (Q-Tip) trust can only be used by spouses and is especially useful for remarried couples. Its main purpose is to postpone payment of estate taxes that would otherwise be due when one spouse dies. But it has an added advantage: It allows you to make certain your spouse has the full or partial use of your property for as long as he or she lives, but permits you to name the ultimate beneficiaries when your spouse dies.

The Discretionary Trust

When there's a disabled child in the family, planners often suggest a trust that gives the trustee (the person or people managing the trust) discretion to use the principal and income as seen fit to meet the beneficiary's needs. The trustee is not required, however, to expend income or principal for the care, health, and education of the disabled child, so that the child doesn't lose government benefits.

BANK ACCOUNTS CAN BE MADE INTO INFORMAL TRUSTS

There's a little-known estate planning device within banks that's simple and cost-free to establish. Known by a variety of names (informal trusts, pay-on-death accounts, bank trust accounts, and Totten trusts, to name a few), these accounts allow you complete control over the funds in them for as long as you live. You can establish a new account with this trust designation or you can convert an existing account. All you do is set up an account in your name listing you as depositor and as "trustee for the benefit of (your beneficiary)." After you die, all the beneficiary needs to do to get the money is present the bank with proof of his or her identity and a certified copy of your death certificate.

Keep in mind that while this trust avoids probate, it is still part of your taxable estate and will not save on federal or state death taxes if your estate is large enough to have to pay them.

JOINT TENANCY AVOIDS PROBATE, BUT...

We talked about joint tenancy with the right of survivorship in the chapter on homes, because residences bought by married couples are frequently owned this way. But bank accounts, even businesses can be owned as joint tenants. And that means when one joint tenant dies, his or her ownership share is automatically transferred to the surviving joint tenant, without having to go through the probate process.

Owning property as a joint tenant doesn't eliminate the property from your taxable estate. However, if husband and wife are joint tenants, only one-half of the value of the joint tenancy property is included in the taxable estate of the first spouse to die.

There are other tax concerns, though, the most important being the federal income tax basis rules. The concepts are complex and differ depending on whether you live in a community property state. They need to be examined with an accountant or estate planner. The general rule of thumb is that it doesn't pay, tax-wise, to transfer substantially appreciated property (or property that *may* substantially appreciate) into joint tenancy with your spouse if you're likely to be the first to die.

LIFE INSURANCE IS A BOON

Life insurance is a wonderful estate planning tool. It's a simple and inexpensive way to protect all the dependents of young stepfamilies (assuming you're in good health and do not have to pay an inflated premium). As I mentioned before, it's also a way of avoiding probate, because the proceeds of the policy go directly to the beneficiary named in the policy. That's important because after your death there will be bills to pay and lost income. Your beneficiary will probably need the ready cash.

Since the proceeds are not subject to probate, only the executor of your estate needs to know about the money so he or she can file the federal estate-tax return. Sometimes the less known the better, especially in remarriages when there may be resentment among children about what their biological parent is leaving to his or her spouse. The law considers husbands and wives one financial entity and says you can move property—in life as in death—to each other free of estate or gift tax. That includes life insurance proceeds.

Proceeds from life insurance are generally income tax free—no matter if you or someone else owns the policy on your life. If you, the insured, own the policy, the proceeds are considered part of your estate, which may mean, depending on the size of the estate, that estate taxes might have to be paid if the beneficiary or beneficiaries are anyone but your spouse. If you don't own the policy (say your children own a policy on your life), the proceeds from the policy are still not subject to income taxes and may escape estate taxes.

Insurance solves problems. Suppose, for example, an older man marries a younger woman about the age of his children. He and she have children together. The husband wants his wife and second family to inherit most of his estate. The problem is that estate consists primarily of stock in his family business, and the wife doesn't want to be involved in the business.

While alive, the husband transfers some equity to his older children who are working in the business. This can be done without losing control. Insurance fills in the rest of the puzzle. The husband buys a large insurance policy on his life naming the wife as beneficiary. He leaves his share of the business to his adult children. There might be a large estate tax on the value of the business (the children can take out insurance on the father to cover the tax due), but his wife is free of estate tax.

Or perhaps a stepfather wants to leave money to his stepchildren without his children knowing about it. If the stepchildren are owners of the life insurance policy (the stepfather can always give them money to cover the cost of the premiums), proceeds from the policy are kept out of his taxable estate.

Insurance is a quiet way of leaving money to heirs.

There's little doubt about the value of insurance in estate planning. The dilemma usually revolves around what kind to buy. Consider this rule of thumb: If a person expects to hold the insurance for less than ten years, he or she should buy term. Longer than that, consider permanent insurance.

Term Insurance

Term, the cheapest form of coverage, provides a preset amount of cash if the insured dies while the policy is in force. If you live beyond the term of the policy (and don't or can't renew it), that's it. No money. It doesn't build up a recoverable cash value. Term is excellent for people with young families because the younger the insured, the more reasonable the premiums. As you get older, there's a steep increase in the rates because you have a greater chance of dying.

Choose a policy that will be renewable at the end of it term, in case you want to keep it in force. If you think you'll want to convert a term policy into a whole life or universal policy some day, look for that feature.

Whole Life
This type of insurance, which goes by a slew of other names (most frequently "straight life") supplies a set amount of coverage for fixed, uniform premiums—but also has a savings feature, called a cash reserve, which earns interest. While you're living, you can cash in or borrow against the reserve.

Compared to term insurance, whole life requires a much greater outlay when you're in your twenties, thirties or forties. There comes a point, though, (and it differs company by company) when whole life's flat rate is less than term's increasing premiums. That's why it doesn't pay to buy whole life for just a few years when you're under forty.

Universal Life
A hybrid of term and whole life, universal, like whole life, builds up a cash reserve at competitive interest rates. But it's flexible. You can vary premium payments or the amount of coverage, or both, from year to year, which is a boon to most remarrieds because each year's financial picture can be so different.

GIFTS TO MINOR CHILDREN

If you're a person who's both financially secure and generous, you can reduce your estate by distributing part of it to your own minor children or stepchildren. Except for a small amount (between $2,500 and $5,000, depending on the state), any property given to a minor must be supervised by an adult. If the gift is for your own child who is living with your former spouse with whom you have a good relationship, the simplest way to make the gift is to give it to the custodial parent outright. Says one Philadelphia nurse remarried for the third time, "Just because I found my first husband frightfully boring doesn't mean he isn't a good father. Nobody cares more about my kids than he does."

Or you could establish a simple trust, say a bank account, under the terms in the Uniform Transfers to Minors Act in your state. As soon as you transfer these funds, however, they are locked in. The account belongs to and is taxed to the child. You can't withdraw the money if you need it, and the funds can only be used for the child's welfare while he or she is a minor. After that, the money is the child's to do with as she or he chooses.

You can also make gifts to stepchildren and biological children this way. And you can also choose anyone to be trustee—your former spouse, your present spouse, even a grandparent.

There are also some investments for children that make tax sense: zero-coupon bonds, stock, and Series I U.S. Savings bonds. The savings bonds have become a real lifesaver in the saving-for-college struggle. If that's the motive behind the gift, buy them for yourself (if you're the parent), your spouse (if you're the stepparent) or your children (if you're the grandparent). If the bonds are cashed in during the year that college tuition is being paid, the parent may not have to pay tax on the accumulated interest, assuming his or her adjusted gross income is not too high).

Keep in mind that you can give annual gifts of up to $10,000 per person to as many people as you want without having to pay any gift tax.

WHAT TO TELL THE KIDS

Death may be a difficult subject for adults to talk about, but it's the stuff of nightmares for children. Most experts suggest talking to school-age children only about the aspects of your death that might concern them, like responding to the question of "Who's going to take care of me if you die, Mommy or my stepmother Sheila?" The details of a will or estate plan are too complicated and would only raise the level of anxiety, so don't share those.

When children are older, they might be asked to share their thoughts. For example, you might sound a fourteen-year-old out on whether he'd want to live with his stepfather or Aunt Jen. Tapping into the children's thoughts doesn't mean you're necessarily going to abide by their wishes. It means you'll consider their opinions when making your decisions.

FITTING THE PIECES TOGETHER

One Family's His-and-Their Children
"It took us about a year to smooth out the rough edges in our individual plans," says Samantha, a 38-year-old Illinois mother of toddler who has been married to Dick for seven years. "And I'm certain that in a few years we'll have to revamp them again. But for now I'm comfortable we've done what we have to do to meet our goals.

"If one of us dies, the other inherits the other's whole estate, and, of course, would be responsible for taking care of our child. Dick also has a $100,000 insurance policy naming the children from his first marriage as beneficiaries.

"We had the most difficult time figuring out what to do if we died simultaneously—or almost simultaneously. Here's what we decided. All that we own jointly—and that's just about everything of value, like our home, cars, and mutual funds—will be split in half. Dick's estate will be divided into three

equal shares for his three children [two from a former marriage and one from the remarriage]. Mine will remain intact for our son, who will need more money for a longer period of time than Dick's children, who are already in their teens. We've named my sister as our son's guardian.

"But there's more," Samantha explains. "Dividing the property that way in our wills left me emotionally uneasy because Dick's daughter has been living with us for the past three years and I've grown very close to her. I wanted to leave her something just from me. So I opened up a bank account in trust for her, which I add small sums to form time to time."

Dick and Samantha stripped together four elements—wills, bank accounts, joint tenancy, and insurance—to come out with viable estate plan.

One Entrepreneur and His Assets

Perry has substantially more money than Linda, primarily because he has a successful dry cleaning store in Seattle. His son from his first marriage had just entered the business when he and Linda married four years ago. With the exception of a $100,000 CD and the $250,000 condo he and Linda bought together, most of his money is tied up in the business.

Perry had two concerns when he redrafted his will: making certain that Linda was well provided for in case of his death (she has no living parents and no children) and leaving the business to his son. Working with his attorney and insurance broker, he entered into a buy-sell agreement that would ensure the sale of the business to his son when he died. The son would fund the agreement by buying life insurance on his father's life so he could pay the estate (which was left to Linda) the fixed buyout price. Every year Perry makes a cash gift to his son to cover the cost of the insurance premium. This estate plan assures him that his son will get the business and Linda will have a large pool of liquid assets.

Money Versus Things: How to Even It Out
One would think that John and Emily Visher, the Dr. Spocks of stepfamilies and co-founders of the Stepfamily Association of America, who have been married for almost forty years, would be able to reach decisions easily when it comes to who gets what. But they admitted that even thirty years into their most successful marriage, they, too, had to do some creative thinking with regard to inheritance. They discovered they had a problem with their estate plan. After putting "her stuff," "his stuff," and "their stuff" on three imaginary table, "her stuff" consisted of valuable family heirlooms, while his table looked pretty bare.

They pondered on how they were going to even things out. "After speaking to the [adult] children, we came up with this solution," John says. "We're going to try to balance out the inequity in our wills by leaving the children different amounts of cash. Hopefully, Emily's four children and my three will feel they have been treated fairly."

TIMES FOR REVISIONS

Just as the process of bringing up children needs mid-course corrections from time to time, estate planning is a process that needs updating or periodic revising. The trigger times for revision are when:

1. Your circumstances change considerably.
2. Your net worth climbs so high that it will probably be subject to an estate tax.
3. You or one of your beneficiaries develops a serious health problem, perhaps an ongoing one that will drain the family of money.
4. You have children—or more children. You need to take their needs into consideration.

5. You want to change the personal guardian you have named for your children.

6. An heir marries, has children, becomes estranged, or dies.

7. Tax laws affecting estates change in ways that will affect you or your heirs.

8. You divorce.

9. You move to a different state. (This review is especially necessary if you move from a common law property state to a community property state or vice versa.)

KEEPING TRACK OF EVERYTHING

Now that you've put your estate in order, it's time to do the same with your papers. Most people keep important papers and possessions scattered in different places—a safe-deposit box, file cabinets, home safes, desk drawers, even dresser drawers. It's hard enough to remember where we put something a year ago. Think of how hard it would be for your heirs if they had to go on a document hunt after you die. It might be years before they find all the important information.

Use the "Paper Trail" worksheet to keep track of your estate planning documents as well as your important financial records. Then make three copies. Send one to the executor of your estate, one to a beneficiary, and keep the third in a desk drawer.

PAPER TRAIL WORKSHEET

For _____ and _____

Social Security #s _____ and _____

Legend:

1 = Safe-deposit box _____ at _____
                           (number)   (bank and address)

2 = Home safe or cabinet

3 = Office safe or cabinet

4 = Lawyer _____ at _____
                        (name)   (firm and address)

5 = Metal box at home in the _____
                                   (location)

6 = Desk at home or in office

7 = At bank _____
                 (name of bank/person to contact/address)

8 = At brokerage _____

9 = Accountant _____at _____
                   (name)   (firm and address)

10 = In computer _____
                 (under what program/file)

Use the legend to
Indicate the location for   Item

Husband	Wife	
_____	_____	Original Will
_____	_____	Copy of will
_____	_____	Living will documents
_____	_____	Letters of last instructions
_____	_____	Personal letters to be distributed after death

_____	_____	Trust agreements
_____	_____	Life insurance policies
_____	_____	Health insurance material
_____	_____	Property and casualty policies
_____	_____	Annuity contracts
_____	_____	Title to car and insurance policies
_____	_____	Deed to home
_____	_____	Safe combinations or keys
_____	_____	Bank records
_____	_____	Checkbooks
_____	_____	Savings and loan records and accounts
_____	_____	Tax records
_____	_____	Record of debts owed to and owed by you
_____	_____	Employment contracts
_____	_____	Corporate retirement plans
_____	_____	Stock option plans
_____	_____	Keogh or IRA plans
_____	_____	Partnership agreements
_____	_____	List of credit cards
_____	_____	Stock, bond, and brokerage records
_____	_____	Mutual fund records
_____	_____	Other real estate deeds
_____	_____	Other investments
_____	_____	Powers of attorney
_____	_____	Health proxies
_____	_____	Cemetery plot deed
_____	_____	Other

Congratulations! You've cleared the hardest psychological hurdle of the financial planning process—estate planning. Having successfully grappled with some of the most complex and emotional questions, you should be able to face other financial challenges with the confidence of an Olympian.

Chapter Eleven

With This Checklist, I Thee Wed

THE FINANCIAL ACTION PLAN

- Establish a joint bank account.
- Rent a safe-deposit box in joint name.
- Update your W-4 forms to reflect the new number of dependents (if that's changing).
- If there's a name or address change, notify Social Security, the IRS, the motor vehicle bureau, credit card companies, and employers.
- Rethink your tax situation and make necessary adjustments.
- Review insurance coverage—life, disability, car and home.
- Change beneficiary designations on life insurance, pension or profit sharing plans and bank accounts.
- Coordinate medical and hospital benefits.
- Reevaluate investments.
- Sift through financial files.

This is an exciting time—the beginning of life as a married couple. Together you will set a financial course for yourselves. Some of the turns are sharper on this course because of the complexity of remarriage; some are easily negotiable because you've been around them before. Buying your new bed, renting a safe-deposit box or working out a preliminary financial plan for two are groundbreaking and, yes, romantic activities.

Many of the financial decisions made as a couple are evolutionary ones, like deciding on a comprehensive estate plan. But the ones in the checklist beginning this chapter are not. To keep you on a straight financial course, they should be done either right before or right after remarriage.

DESIGNATE AN "OURS" BANK

Assuming you're going to have a joint account, set it up at a bank that's convenient to both of you. (This doesn't preclude each of you from having your own accounts elsewhere). This "household" account gives each of you easy access to deposit and withdraw money. Rent a joint safe-deposit box at this bank as well, into which you transfer all your important papers (separation and divorce decrees, marriage and birth certificates, stock certificates, titles to cars, homes, etc.)

Formulate a provisional plan for (1) who's going to be responsible for paying bills from the account, (2) a financial recordkeeping system, (3) what will be paid out of the joint account, and (4) how much each partner can withdraw without discussing it with the other.

TAXES FOR TWO

Wedding Time
If you have the choice between getting married in December of January, factor in taxes before you decide.

If one of you has considerably less income than the other, opt for December. You'll generally be taxed less if you're married and filing jointly than you would be if each of you filed separate returns.

If both of you have about the same income, choose January. There's a glitch in the tax code that penalizes married couples who earn approximately the same income. They often pay more tax than if they filed two single returns.

Dependency Exemption.
Child custody arrangements affect taxes. Here's how it works. The parent who has custody of a child for the greater part of the year claims the exemption, no matter how little he or she contributes toward the child's financial support. (This practice continues through college. The child can be claimed as a dependent if your home continues to be his or her primary residence.) If, as a result of your remarriage, you child comes to live with you and your new spouse for most of the year, you can take the dependency exemption on your tax return—even if your separation agreement says something else. The only way the IRS recognizes a different arrangement is if the spouse usually claiming the dependency exemption signs a form waiving his or her right to this exemption. Then you have to attach it to your return. (Be certain only one parent claims the exemption. You'll wind up owing additional taxes and penalties if the deduction is disallowed.)

Moving Deduction
A tax deduction available to people who move and change jobs as a result of the remarriage might be a surprise. Moving expenses incurred as a result of switching jobs, if the location of your new job is at least thirty-five miles farther from your residence than your old job, are often tax deductible—assuming you find another job rather quickly.

Here's the employment test. If you're an employee, you must be working full time at your new job location for at least fifty weeks of the twelve-month period that follows your move to the new location.

If you're self-employed, there's an additional requirement. You must work full time as either an employee or a self-employed person at your new job location for at least seventy-eight weeks of the twenty-four-month period following your move.

The employment requirement obviously is waived in the event of your death or disability. It's also waived if you're fired, laid off or transferred for reasons other than willful misconduct.

IRAS

Tax laws regarding IRAs (tax-deductible ones and Roth IRAs) are constantly changing, so it's important to check with your accountant or tax professional to find out just how much money can be put into an IRA each year.

Inequity of Tax Payments

Discuss how you're going to handle tax payments when you're married and filing jointly. This becomes a consideration, especially when one spouse is earning considerably more than the other is. Ellen and Kurt are a good example of the problem. Ellen earns $40,000 a year. When she was single she filed as a head of household and was in a low tax bracket. Kurt earns over $100,000 and is in the highest tax bracket. Now that they're married, they're filing a joint return. Ellen knows she can't afford to split the tax indebtedness with Kurt; Kurt doesn't expect it.

They've looked at two possibilities. The simplest would be to apply the ratio of their income to their share of the taxes. That means Ellen would contribute about 30 percent of the tax bill, and Kurt about 70 percent.

But the income tax system is progressive, so a simple proportion may not be equitable. Another arrangement, fairer in absolute terms, is that Ellen would not pay more taxes married than she would have paid if she were filing as she had before as a head of household.

ADDITIONAL RESPONSIBILITY, ADDITIONAL INSURANCE

Step over the threshold of your new remarriage and tumbling in with you are more kids, more cars, more pets, and more family and friends.

Financial translation: More, or different, insurance.

Homeowner's Insurance

If one of you is moving into the other's home, the additional furniture, electronic equipment and "stuff" means you need more homeowner's coverage, because the policy covers the home and its contents. Grab a notebook. You'll have to do a personal property inventory to determine the amount of coverage needed. The inventory also helps you settle a claim if a loss occurs. You might want to add a personal property floater policy to extend protection to expensive personal items, such as heirloom jewelry, that are otherwise slighted in a standard homeowner's policy.

Renters, too, need property insurance. Landlords are held liable for losses to your property only if you can prove they were negligent—like by not providing the doorman security promised.

Liability Coverage

With more people traipsing in and out of the house, there's an increased chance of an accident in which someone is hurt. So consider increasing the liability portion of your homeowner's insurance, or if you think you're a prime target for large liability claims because of your combined incomes, purchase an umbrella policy that increases liability coverage to one million dollars or more for homeowner's and automobile insurance.

Life Insurance

Do you need additional life insurance to protect your new spouse? Probably. If your divorce agreement mandates that you keep a policy with a former spouse as beneficiary, you must abide by that. It doesn't work to change the beneficiary designation on that policy to your new spouse because when you die, your former spouse could sue and collect under the terms of the divorce or separation agreement. That would leave your spouse with hefty legal bills but no insurance.

Disability Insurance

Few married couples can afford the loss of one income for any significant period, so if you aren't already covered, waste no time in getting disability insurance. At age thirty-five, the chance of becoming seriously disabled for three months or more is nearly three times as great as the chance of dying. At fifty, the odds are nearly four times as great.

Social security disability insurance is helpful only in the most extreme cases, and though some large companies provide employees with disability insurance, most do not. So you may be forced to get private insurance that will replace 60 to 70 percent of your income.

Look for policies that (1) allow you to boost your coverage if your income increases, (2) can't be canceled as long as you pay your premium, (3) will provide coverage if you can't do the type of work you're used to doing—not just if you can't do any work, (4) will allow you to ease back into work without losing all your benefits, and (5) have automatic cost-of-living increases. To shave premiums, stretch the elimination period, the time between when income stops and benefits begin, for as long as your personal resources will allow.

Automobile Insurance

Car insurance probably will need updating. In some cases there might be a savings. The insurance on three cars registered at one address, for example, usually costs less than the sum of the premiums on two cars insured in one household and one car in another. On the other hand, if your spouse comes with a daredevil teenage driver, rates could skyrocket.

CHANGE BENEFICIARIES

Life insurance policies often need to have the beneficiary changed. You probably will remember to do that for the policy you own individually, but don't forget group policies taken out by your employer.

Change the beneficiary designations on your pensions, Keogh plans, and IRAs. A former spouse may still have rights to a retirement account during the first year of a remarriage unless you change the beneficiary.

MERGE BENEFITS

Working husbands and wives come to this marriage toting two separate benefits packages. What better time than right now to weed out duplicate coverage and maximize benefits?

Health and Medical Insurance. If each of you is covered under a group insurance plan that covers 80 percent of your medical expenses, consider adding each other and all the dependent children to both plans. After you file and your claim in reimbursed (up to 80 percent), your spouse files with his or her plan to collect the remaining 20 percent. Your plans work together to provide up to 100 percent of your expenses.

If one of you is in an HMO, you might be better off covering the two adults and all dependent children under that. Whatever combination of plans you're bringing to the remarriage, examine how they dovetail or overlap with each other.

401(k) Plans. Which of you has an employer matching contributions to a 401(k) plan? If one of you doesn't have that perk and the other does, there's no doubt as to which plan should receive most or all of your joint retirement savings. The person without matching funds should stop contributing to the plan, thereby increasing his or her take-home pay. If the other spouse increases his or her contribution to the 401(k), the couple comes out ahead.

Consider immediate needs. Don't stash away money you're going to need now. If you wind up withdrawing money meant for retirement (from IRAs, Keoghs, 401(k)s or pension plans) earlier than age fifty-nine-and-a-half, you'll pay a 10 percent penalty, and the IRS will count the funds as taxable income in the year they're withdrawn.

Choose your benefits. If you have a flexible benefit plan at work, one which allows you a choice of benefits, coordinate coverage with your spouse. You might be able to trade vacation days for money or vice versa, depending on the family needs at the moment. Be wary about dropping medical coverage if your spouse's job isn't deadbolt secure, however. You could run into problems if you try to reinstate medical coverage.

REVIEW INVESTMENTS

Whether you plan to merge your investments or maintain separate portfolios, give your investments the once-over early in your marriage so that you can begin to create a workable, diversified, intelligent "family" package—one you both understand and could handle in case one of you has to take over management for the other.

The investments people bring to a remarriage may not be as colorful as their plaid armchairs and scarlet sofas, but they usually "fit" their owners well. Just as there is no perfect chair, there is no right investment. Right depends upon who you are—your age, occupation, number and needs of dependents, health, investment knowledge, insurance coverage, net worth, and your ability to feel at ease with your holdings (your "risk comfort level"). Suppose one of you has a vast knowledge of the economy and investment markets. At any given time, that spouse may own shares in growth and single-country mutual funds and have gold coins in the vault. The less sophisticated of you may be glued to two investments: bank CDs and Treasury notes. Who's going to make more money over a given period of time? Nobody knows. "Even when the experts all agree, they may well be mistaken," Bertrand Russell said. Individually, neither the sophisticated risk taker nor the conservative, risk-averse investor in this example has a solidly diversified portfolio. As a couple, however, the extreme positions provide ballast for one another.

Risk Wisely

Remarriage is risky. Yet you're not going to give up this relationship because the risk is great. By reading this book, you're already decreasing the risk that your remarriage will fail. You're arming yourself with knowledge and strategies for meeting its challenges and successfully negotiating them.

Investing is risky, too. But just as remarriage can be richly rewarding, investing can be also, as long as it's carefully thought out. Taking too much risk is misguided; so is taking too little. Ditch the idea that there's a perfectly risk-free investment. Even the honorable Treasury bond can be a loser if you're locked into it at an annual interest rate of 5 percent during a time when the inflation rate is a soaring 12 percent.

How do you cut the rate of failure when risking money? What's a prudent, thought-out risk?

1. *Look for an investment with a high probability of return.* While nothing is guaranteed, an investment that doesn't have an all-or-nothing

bottom line and gives you opportunity to sell it at a later date (if that's what you choose to do) is your best bet.

2. *Balance your portfolio* so that you have diversity and liquidity (money available for almost-instant use) between the two spouses.

3. *Set simple plans in motion that will keep your investments growing.* The early years of remarriage are often chaotic. For those who don't have long stretches of time to develop investment strategies, or for those who aren't interested in becoming investment gurus, consider some painless, almost automatic, ways to keep accumulating investment dollars.

- An automatic payroll deduction plan, where your employer deducts a set amount from your paycheck and transfers it to a money market account or savings plan. If your company doesn't have such a plan, banks do. With your authorization, they'll subtract a stipulated amount from your checking account on a predetermined date and transfer it into a money market account.

- Reinvesting the dividends you receive as a shareholder in a public company or mutual fund, or as a bondholder. Call your broker or check the company's literature for how to set the reinvestment process in motion automatically.

- An installment plan technique called dollar-cost averaging. Each month you invest a set amount in a particular mutual fund, for example. The amount is always the same whether the price of the shares is up or down. Over time, you're likely to accumulate more shares at a median price than at high prices. For example, one month $100 will buy ten shares of a mutual fund selling at $10 per share and the next month it will buy fourteen shares at $7.15 a share. You wind up with twenty-four shares at an average price of $8.33 under dollar-cost averaging.

SORT, SAVE AND DUMP FINANCIAL RECORDS

It's best if you can sift through financial records before remarriage so you don't have to pay movers to cart files that you'll wind up throwing out later. Here's what to keep and what to toss:

Income Tax Records
In general, the IRS has three years from the date your return is due to challenge it. So keep your 2000 return (filed in April of 2001) until 2004, and so on.

But....audit time limits are extended to six years if the IRS can show that you failed to report income exceeding 25 percent of what you reported. If there's any possibility of that, hold your returns and the back-up material for six years.

All bets are off if fraud is involved. There's no statute of limitations then.

Keep your tax records
- 3 years—if your income consists only of interest earnings and wages reported on a W-2.
- 6 years—if you're an independent contractor reporting business income on Schedule C.
- Forever—if there could be any doubt about the veracity of your return.

Home Records
Save all the receipts for home improvements and repairs, such as the purchase of a new boiler, patio or bathroom renovations, the installation of central air conditioning or building of a new wing. Anything that can be added to your home's purchase price to increase its cost basis is useful because with the enormous increase in property value in some areas, you

might find yourself faced with some tax, if you exceed $250,000 in profits ($500,000 for couples) when you sell your house.

Keep the information on the latest assessment on your home. Keep the cancelled checks for any property taxes paid.

Retirement Accounts

Trash all but the most recent quarterly reports of transactions and annuity benefits reports. But keep—indefinitely—records pertaining to nondeductible IRA contributions.

Divorce Decrees and Death Certificates

For at least the first few years of a remarriage, keep all the papers and letters from a former spouse that might be relevant in the event of any court proceedings. When animosities abate and your former spouse seems to have gotten on with his or her life, that's the time to toss them. Keep the separation and divorce decree forever, however. The same holds true for the death certificate of a former spouse.

Investments

The "toss" list:

- Expired CDs (once you receive Tax Form 1099 and verify the interest earning reported)
- All but the most recent money market account statements and the one for past December (which gives you the tax information you'll need to file your return in April)
- Annual reports of companies in which you own stock and shareholders' reports on your mutual funds (once you've read them)
- All but the first and last prospectuses from mutual funds in which you have invested money, and all but your latest cumulative report on transactions and the December year-end cumulative report

- The quarterly distribution statements of limited partnerships (but keep your original prospectus and K-1 tax forms)

  The "keep" list:
- Confirmations of all purchases and redemptions of stocks and bonds for as long as you own them. When you sell, keep the papers for as long as you retain tax records. Also keep a record of dividends that have been reinvested.
- Tax Form 8583 for passive activity loss limitations. If you can't deduct passive losses, such as from rental real estate, keep this form until the property is sold, when those losses can be claimed.

Bank Records

Keep cancelled checks and bank statements for as long as you keep tax returns. (Once you've checked deposit slips against the statement, however, you can toss them.) The procedure changes with savings accounts. For these you need keep only the latest statement and the one for the previous December.

Unless you use them as backup for a tax deduction or a warranty, keep credit card monthly statements for only a year.

Automobiles

Keep the purchase order and title and confirmation of a car loan you paid off (Just in case there's still a record of a lien on it when you sell the car). Also keep the car's maintenance records (so you can give them to the new owner when you sell it) and your most recent registration and insurance papers. Toss all other papers relating to the car.

Insurance

Scrap cancelled or outdated policies—car, home or life. Keep only current policies.

Hold onto only the most recent copies of annuity and cash value reports relating to life policies.

Information relating to car and home claims settled more than a year ago can be tossed.

Medical and dental insurance reimbursement statements should be kept for at least a year. If you're going to be taking a tax deduction for medical expenses, keep the records (and the medical bills) for as long as you keep you tax records.

If you change jobs, keep the summary of medical coverage from your previous employer for a year to track coverage of pre-existing conditions in case you have to settle old claims.

Odds and Ends
Keep Tax Form 942, which records paying Social Security tax and Federal unemployment insurance for household employees, just in case a former employee asserts, sometime in the future, that you didn't make the required contributions.

Toss—expired warranties, phone and utility bills over a year old (unless they are part of the home office deduction you're taking on a tax return), and all but your most recent and the previous December's pay stubs.

Remarriage presents a rare opportunity to start again, to right what was wrong with the financial arrangements of a former life, to turn chaos into order. Use the Financial Action Plan to make this an easy and enlightened time of financial transition.

Chapter Twelve

Conclusion

The American family is a remarried family. Call us blended, reconstituted, step. Whatever our designation, we're the contemporary American family.

Picture these images of financial woes. Don't they look close even when viewed from a safe distance?

- A husband and wife seated at a dining room table strewn with papers, bills, statements and checkbooks, poring over a phone bill. They're clearly in a snit over the long distance calls each of their children have made to the other biological parent—one in Dallas, one in Chicago.
- A man stuffing an envelope addressed to his former spouse into a mailbox. He's glaring. In his mind it's clearly marked "alimony." His wife stands next to him and she looks peeved. It's hard to know if her annoyance is directed at her husband or the recipient of the envelope.
- A harried husband and wife coming home from work being met by four children—two teenage boys (obviously his), one teenage girl (obviously hers), and a toddler who looks like both of them. One boy is grabbing for the keys to a car, the other is holding up a piece of paper indicating how much his hockey uniform will cost, the girl pointing to a picture of a computer with pleading eyes, and the toddler is crying because he doesn't want his babysitter to leave.

Narrowly focusing on the sometimes gloomy, confusing or bizarre financial situations we find ourselves in, we can make the mistake of losing the background against which these remarital scenes are set. In a committed remarriage, the backdrop is one of adventure and love. A sense of humor serves as a telephoto lens. It helps isolate a ridiculous, hilarious or ludicrous moment. Increasing exposure by taking more time to view the scene is the major ally in lightening up the picture—and your perspective.

I now have the time to look back on how we handled our finances in the first, say seven, years of our remarriage. Let me share with you some of what we did wrong:

- I like resolution, so every time we closed our bedroom door to "discuss" my anxiety about our precarious financial position, I expected we'd emerge two hours later with a solution in hand. My expectations were unreal.

- I assumed too many of the financial chores. In my first marriage I had abdicated almost all of the financial responsibilities. When I divorced, I felt I'd been financially scalded because, among other things, of my monetary nincompoopery. In my "never again" mode, I mistook scut work for control.

- We didn't do a budget overview until years after we were married. The whole idea of accounting for every expenditure was abhorrent to both of us. Neither could we stand thinking of ourselves as detail people. While my husband felt comfortable enough with his mental math, I didn't. I wallowed in worry without knowing if there was reason for it.

We're not through with our financial work yet. In addition to the evolutionary and ongoing future decisions we'll have to make, we still haven't done some of what we should have.

We haven't thrown away the yellowing tax record of the 70s and 80s cluttering the closet shelves.

We've stopped budgeting on paper. We earn more than we spend and are able to save a small percentage of our total annual income. Good enough. Maybe, one day, we'll go back to it, but for now budgeting is strictly mental gymnastics to be engaged in…whenever.

We're still noodling around on long term insurance. This "should we or shouldn't we" debate has been going on for the past four years.

I don't consider any of these grievous problems, however.

It's what we've done right, after some bumbling starts, that will, in the long run, best serve our marriage. And we're not alone. The underlying threads that run through the stories of every successfully remarried couple I interviewed for this book are the same.

- They are tenacious about problem-solving. If one "solution" proves elusive, they try another. The pieces to the puzzle are all there, they reason. Their job is to keep trying to put them together.
- They communicate and negotiate. They spend so much time talking, listening, and yes, even screaming about financial differences that they finally learned to hear one another.
- They subscribe to the philosophy of "what's important to you is important to me." That doesn't mean agreeing. It means respecting differences.
- They have been determined to make the marriage work because they care deeply about one another.

Like the ingredients in Grandma's special cake, the ingredients for financial compatibility can't be measured. Each couple creates its own personal blend, depending on such standard financial factors as priorities, needs, obligations, goals and the amount of money available. The spices—whether you're a free spender or a freeloader, a complainer or a coper, or whether you money motivation is power, love, security or freedom—will add flavor and interest to your financial future as a couple.

For my husband and me, it's twenty-five and counting. Our understanding of how to manage a financial union has evolved over time.

We've made it clear to each other what we can't live with and have been discovering what we want to live with, what we enjoy living with. He still thinks it's overkill to traipse to nine different dealerships in four counties over a period of three weekends just to negotiate a $500 price break on a car. I have a nagging feeling it's important. But I don't chastise him as a careless spender, nor does he castigate me with taunts of "cheapskate." We just have different styles and have learned to compromise. Last time we bought a new car it meant comparing prices of cars online and the next two weekends visiting dealers generated by our online search. We paid $1,400 off the list price. Better still, we walked away hand in hand and pleased with ourselves—even though we'll never know if we had the best deal in four counties.

Though nobody denies it's better to have enough money than to brood about how you're going to earn the next dollar or spend every cent, wealth doesn't necessarily pave the way for a rich remarriage. Kristine, who was a buyer with a major department store in San Francisco when she married Charlie eight years ago, described what has made her marriage so rich.

"I knew Charlie was dedicated to upholding the major financial commitment he had to his first wife and two children," she says. "And I suspected that he wouldn't be able to contribute much to hour household initially because at the time he was only a moderately recognized artist with a fluctuating income. But since I was well paid, we didn't feel the pinch.

"Then I became pregnant," Kristine says. "When I was in my sixth month, Charlie was offered a job in the art department of a major movie studio. The salary was spectacular and would have put us in another ballpark. Charlie wavered. He hated the idea of reporting to someone who would criticize his work based on commercial standards, but he knew I wanted to be home with the baby and he didn't want me to worry about our finances. 'We're going to have a baby. I have to consider it,' he said. We agonized over the offer because, in reality, I was worried about money. I could see that as much as he wanted to provide me with peace of mind, this job would stifle him. When I finally said,

'*I think this is wrong for you and I don't want you to take it just for me,' he was visibly moved…and relieved.*"

That was three years and two babies ago. Kristine hasn't gone back to retailing yet. "*At first, I resented his former wife because of the money she was getting for child support. Then I wondered about the wisdom of our job decisions because we had to cut back our spending considerably,*" she continues. "*But I don't wonder anymore. Having children myself makes me more empathetic to his former wife's needs. As for Charlie's work, he's become a well-known and sought-after artist. I'm thrilled, of course. But it's more than that. If I had had to face a resentful many every night—no matter how well he tried to hide it—we wouldn't be married anymore. Instead, when Charlie comes home from his studio, I'm greeted by a fulfilled person who shows me in many different ways how thankful he is that I didn't pressure him into a nine-to-five job.*"

An exciting aspect of marriage is that personally and as a couple you can redefine your financial goals. Though the definition of what makes a financially successful couple is subjective, the path to achieving harmony is simple—if at times easier to read about than to follow. It rests on two principles. This relationship is worth having and this relationship is worth working for. Over the years you build on that, learning to communicate your financial feelings and needs, respecting each other's differences, negotiating and compromising when appropriate, and behaving as financial equals.

These are the investments in a remarriage. With each, financial unity compounds. Per annum, the financial relationship swells with a wealth that is one part money, one part trust, and one part love.

Printed in the United States
44383LVS00003B/169

9 780595 169092